MATTHEW

The Teacher's Gospel

Paul S. Minear

1 The book of the genealogy of Jesus Christ, the son of David, the son of Abraham.

2 Abraham was the father of Isaac, and Isaac the father of Jacob, and Jacob the father of Judah and his brothers, 3 and Judah the father of Perez and Zerah by Tamar, and Perez the father of Hezron, and Hezron the father of Ram,*a* 4 and Ram*a* the father of Ammin′adab, and Ammin′adab the father of Nahshon, and Nahshon the father of Salmon, 5 and Salmon the father of Bo′az by Rahab, and Bo′az the father of Obed by Ruth, and Obed the father of Jesse, 6 and Jesse the father of David the king.

And David was the father of Solomon by the wife of Uri′ah, and Solomon the father of Rehobo′am, and Rehobo′am the father of Abi′jah, and Abi′jah the father of Asa,*b* 8 and Asa*b* the father of Jehosh′aphat, and Jehosh′aphat the father of Joram, and Joram the father of Uzzi′ah, 9 and Uzzi′ah the father of Jotham, and Jotham the father of Ahaz, and Ahaz the father of Hezeki′ah, 10 and Hezeki′ah the father of Manas′seh, and Manas′seh the father of Amos,*c* and Amos*c* the father of Josi′ah, 11 and Josi′ah the father of Jechoni′ah and his brothers, at the time of the deportation to Babylon.

12 And after the deportation to Babylon: Jechoni′ah was the father of She-al′ti-el,*d* and She-al′ti-el*d* the father of Zerub′babel, 13 and Zerub′babel the father of Abi′ud, and Abi′ud the father of Eli′akim, and Eli′akim the father of Azor, 14 and Azor the father of Zadok, and Zadok the father of Achim, and Achim the father of Eli′ud, 15 and Eli′ud the father of Elea′zar, and Elea′zar the father of Matthan, and Matthan the father of Jacob, 16 and Jacob the father of Joseph the husband of Mary, of whom Jesus was born, who is called Christ.

17 So all the generations from Abraham to David were fourteen generations, and from David to the deportation to Babylon fourteen generations, and from the deportation to Babylon to the Christ fourteen generations.

18 Now the birth of Jesus Christ*f* took place in this way. When his mother Mary had been betrothed to Joseph, before they came together she was found to be with child of the Holy Spirit; 19 and her husband Joseph, being a just man and unwilling to put her to shame, resolved to divorce her quietly. 20 But as he considered this, behold, an angel of the Lord appeared to him in a dream, saying, "Joseph, son of David, do not fear to take Mary your wife, for that which is conceived in her is of the Holy Spirit; 21 she will bear a son, and you shall call his name Jesus, for he will save his people from their sins." 22 All this took place to fulfil what the Lord had spoken by the prophet: 23 "Behold, a virgin shall conceive and bear a son,
and his name shall be called Emman′u-el"
(which means, God with us). 24 When Joseph woke from sleep, he did as the angel of the Lord commanded him; he took his wife, 25 but knew her not until she had borne a son; and he called his name Jesus.

a Greek *Asaph*   *c* Other authorities read *Amon*   *d* Greek *Salathiel*
... the meaning of the Christ ... Ruth 4.18-22; 1 Chron. 2.5, 11-15; 1 Kings 4.14; Jer. 27. 20
... Ruth 4.12; 2.21; 1 Chron. 1.29; Acts 10. ...

MATTHEW

The Teacher's
Gospel

MATTHEW

The Teacher's Gospel

PAUL S. MINEAR

The Pilgrim Press
New York

All biblical quotations, unless otherwise indicated, are from the *Revised Standard Version of the Bible,* copyright 1946, 1952, and © 1971 by the Division
of Christian Education, National Council of Churches and are used by permission. The quotation marked NEB is from *The New English Bible* © The
Delegates of the Oxford University Press and the Syndics of the Cambridge
University Press, 1961, 1970. Reprinted with permission. Supplements 1
(1950), 4 (1953), and 6 (1973) are reprinted from *Theology Today* and are
used by permission. Supplement 2 is reprinted with permission from *The
Commands of Christ* by Paul S. Minear. Copyright © 1972 by Abingdon Press.
Supplement 3 is reprinted from *Christian Hope and the Second Coming* by Paul
S. Minear. Copyright, MCMLIV, by W.L. Jenkins. Reprinted by permission
of The Westminster Press. Supplement 5 is reprinted from the 1953 edition
of *Missions Under the Cross*; used by permission of Lutterworth Press (London).

Library of Congress Cataloging in Publication Data

Minear, Paul S., 1906–
   Matthew, the teacher's gospel.

   Bibliography: p. 194
   1. Bible. N.T. Matthew—Criticism,
interpretation, etc. I. Title.
BS2575.2.M56   1982   226′.207   82–10178
ISBN 0-8298-0617-2 (pbk.)

The Pilgrim Press, 132 West 31 Street, New York, New York 10001

To Ruth Minear

lifelong student and teacher
of the Bible

CONTENTS

PREFACE

Most studies of Matthew have been oriented toward a recovery of the portrait of Jesus or toward strengthening faith in him in our time. I have chosen a different orientation. The focus of my attention is on the work of the Evangelist as a teacher and on his intended audience in the churches of the first century—men and women who, like many of us, were charged with basic educational work among adult believers in Jesus Christ. I hope that such an orientation may strengthen your sense of kinship both with the Evangelist, who was a teacher, and with his first readers, who also were teachers.

This study of the Gospel According to Saint Matthew may well be used by men and women who teach adult Bible classes. Therefore, helps for such teachers have been included for each of my chapters; see Appendix A: Notes for Teachers. But nothing in teaching Matthew is more vital than the encouragement among students of an intensive, imaginative, and sustained encounter with the biblical text itself. The preparation for every class session should be a reading and re-reading of a selected segment of this text. I hope my notes for teachers will improve such preparation and thus make discussions more lively. My references to the work of other scholars have been limited to books in English that may be readily accessible in public or college libraries. These books will be helpful, but they should not be allowed to distract attention that should center on the Gospel itself.

Any close study of the Gospel of Matthew should clarify pictures of Jesus and the modern significance of faith in him. On these matters you will find in the supplements positive suggestions that I have extracted from my earlier studies. For permissions to use these extracts I am indebted to the respective editors: *Theology Today,* for Supplements 1, 4, 6; Abingdon Press, for Supplement 2; Westminster Press, for

Supplement 3; Edinburgh House Press, for Supplement 5.

I must also express thanks to the acrobatic fingers of Becci Jagielski, of Fort Worth, Texas, and Effie Good, of Guilford, Connecticut. Happy the author who has such excellent assistance with a recalcitrant manuscript!

So to you who study the Gospel of Matthew I say, Have a good time, with unexpected discoveries, and with exciting discussions with others interested in this Gospel.

MATTHEW

*The Teacher's
Gospel*

Chapter I

INTRODUCTION TO THE GOSPEL

I have chosen the subtitle "The Teacher's Gospel" for a double reason: The author of this Gospel was a *teacher* who designed his work to be of maximum help to *teachers* in Christian congregations. The author is called Matthew, although actually his name is unknown; also unknown are the names of the teachers in his first audience. Yet we know what their basic duties were, and we hope to share this knowledge as we examine successive paragraphs of the Gospel. I hazard the guess that because of Matthew's usefulness as a first textbook for congregational teachers later editors of Christian scriptures usually placed this Gospel first in the New Testament. Its usefulness as a pedagogical summary had continued through nineteen centuries of steady use.

The axis between Matthew and his original readers might be described in the phrase "from one teacher to other teachers." Those teachers today are not seminary or university scholars, but pastors and teachers whose primary responsibility is the instruction of those who have been called as followers of Jesus Christ. I hope to suggest new understandings and appreciations, and perhaps, in turn, these may make teaching more reliable and more effective. To this end I have supplemented the examination of Matthew's text with questions for discussion and projects for exploration.

My aim is to recover—so far as possible—certain lines of conversation that linked Matthew to his original audience. In his own situation the author was not conscious he was editing a document that would later become part of the Holy Bible. Nor were his first readers aware of such a prospect. For them, the law and the prophets formed all the scripture they needed. The message about Christ was important, but it came to them primarily as an oral proclamation concerning momentous events, not as a written document about these events. To reconstruct this early situation may seem to cast doubt on the authority of this document as scripture. Many readers, however, find the opposite to be true; they find their own comprehension of scripture enhanced by a reconstruction of the ancient situation in which a very human leader of the church was impelled to address a very human segment of the community with very specific traditions, drawn from memories and traditions about Jesus. Thus, my initial quest has to do with the identity and character of the author and his audience.

The Author

It is not easy to identify this particular author. Originally, the book lacked a name. Whoever he was, he did not intrude himself into the story. The story was everything; his own prestige, nothing. Scholars have found traces of his peculiar interests, but even the most ingenious detective cannot be sure he or she has found the author's fingerprints, let alone his name. He seems to have looked on himself as a conserver and mediator, rather than as a creator. In fact, we may be dealing with a group of conservers or librarians, rather than with an individual working alone. Even so, within a century of its appearance the document did attract a name but only, it seems, after it had established a firm hold on church loyalties. Certainly Irenaeus attributes this Gospel to Matthew (*Against Heresies* III, 1, 1). Irenaeus was writing about the year A.D. 180, probably depending on Papias who about A.D. 130 had identified Matthew as the writer of certain teachings in Hebrew (Aramaic) language. (It is doubtful if Papias was speaking of the same document.)

Even if the apostle Matthew had been the author (not

likely, but not impossible), knowledge of his name would help us little, because we know virtually nothing else about him. Although four lists include his name among the apostles (Matthew 10:3; Mark 3:18; Luke 6:15; Acts 1:13), only one text provides any information about his background. Here he is described as a collector of taxes, able to entertain Jesus and Jesus' disreputable company at dinner, thereby increasing the hatred directed toward him by Jewish nationalists and religionists (Matthew 9:9f.). Such facts are interesting, but they tell us nothing about the document that, two generations later, began to circulate among the churches. When referring to this book we must continue to use the name Matthew, without implying that the apostle with this name actually wrote it.

When we look for traces of the author's position and motives rather than for his name, the document provides more impressive data. For example, it is clear the author was a follower of Christ—a member of the community of followers, for whom he could and did speak in the first person "we" and "us." To bear the name of Christ was more difficult and decisive then than now in many parts of the modern world. And it is clear this editor accepted wholly the authority Jesus had given his apostles to preach, teach, and heal. He placed himself under the obligation to obey as well as to teach "the least of these commandments" (5:17-20). He accepted the risks and responsibilities of baptism and the Last Supper. As he told each episode in the story and relayed each demand of Jesus, he would have been made aware of the necessity of honesty (5:33-37) and the dangers of hypocrisy (7:15f.). It may have been his humble integrity as a Christian that led him to hide himself so completely behind the story. In any case it is clear he identified himself emotionally not with the Pharisees or the Romans, but with the crowds and the disciples who hailed Jesus as prophet and as the Son of David. He had accepted and had been accepted by the new family of Christ (12:48-50). Therefore, whatever was included in the document was included because of its relevance to this family and to the author. This is so obvious a feature that it is often overlooked.

Another feature of the author's status is almost as certain: Within the church of his day he belonged among the leaders, those who had honored special obligations on the one side to the "Lord" and on the other to his "little ones." It is less easy to specify the types of authority Matthew exercised, but several inferences may be made with some degree of confidence. Among the list of spiritual gifts itemized by Paul (1 Corinthians 12:28f.), the gift of teaching may safely be assigned to Matthew. This vocation probably included the preparation of believers (mostly adult) for baptism (28:16-20) and the continued guidance and instruction of the local community as a whole. Each crisis faced by this community, each debate with hostile groups, each internal altercation among family members would have provided an occasion for a teacher to give specific advices drawn from the legacy of Jesus. It must constantly be remembered that the early church was almost wholly dependent on oral means of communication; few persons knew how to read or write. No books were in general circulation, and teaching was carried on mostly by mouth-to-ear transfers. As a result, the people had developed their powers of memory to a much higher degree than is common in cultures that rely on the written word. The early congregation depended on its teachers to keep its memory active and accurate. These teachers were instrumental in making accessible whatever materials were needed. They had an obligation to both previous and contemporary generations; in Matthew's case this meant he stood between the original company of apostles and his own church. (Matthew's teaching role is reflected in 5:19 and 28:20.)

A third feature of Matthew is also known: As a teacher-scribe, he was probably a converted Jew who had remained, in his own thinking, very much a member of God's people, Israel. Possibly he had earlier been a scribe, then serving the synagogue as he later served the church. Churches in his area may well have seemed to be synagogues comprising those Jews and gentiles who had accepted Jesus as the Messiah. This would explain his extensive knowledge and frequent use of the scriptures; he had a penchant for linking events in the

Gospel story to the Old Testament (e.g., 1:22; 2:15, 17, 23; 4:14; 5:17; 8:17; 12:17; 13:35; 21:4; 26:56; 27:9). His Gospel makes most explicit the understanding of Jesus' commands as fulfilling the law and the prophets (5:17). It also vividly describes the developing impasse between Jesus and the leaders of God's chosen people whom he had come to save (1:21). To Matthew, this controversy with Israel was not incidental, but painful and inescapable. That this scribe's affections lay wholly with the new community is certain. He welcomed the inclusion of gentiles and heartily supported a worldwide mission, based on the revelation of a kingdom in which many—like the Roman centurion—would "sit at table with Abraham, Isaac, and Jacob [8:11]." He had been and remained a Jew; he had been and remained a scribe. Yet he had been radically changed by his enrollment in the followers of Christ and by his own instruction in the mysteries of the kingdom (13:52). This being so, his work within the churches involved him in continuing debates with his former colleagues, the leaders of the synagogues. Thus, he had a personal as well as a professional stake in the accounts of Jesus' debates with the Pharisees.

The Audience

What is known about the initial audience for whom this editor wrote? Like the author, they were all Christians. It is doubtful if they as yet used this title; they probably spoke of themselves simply as those who claimed "the name of Christ" (10:40-42; 18:5, 20; 19:29; 24:9). They belonged to Christ in a strong sense of this verb and found such terms as slaves, brothers, children, and little ones congenial to their new loyalty (18:1-14; 19:13, 14; 5:22-24, 47; 7:3-5; 12:49, 50; 23:8). They did not know Jesus before his death but had come to know him as the living Lord through messengers whom Jesus had commanded to visit the cities of Israel (10:5-23). They had come to believe God had given Jesus "all authority in heaven and on earth [28:18]," despite and even because of the fact he had been repudiated by Israel's rulers and executed by Rome's soldiers. They had accepted baptism in his name, a step that jeopardized their standing in both Jewish and gentile communities, for it associated them with those who had been branded enemies of law, order, and religion. Now they were struggling to find their own patterns of living, distinct from the Pharisees with "their synagogues" and from the gentiles.

Probably this audience was made up largely of Jews who had been persuaded that the agelong hopes of Israel were finally being realized. Each sabbath this worshiping company listened to readings from God's word. The line separating church from synagogue was formed by the answer to the question whether the law and the prophets had been fulfilled in the events that had recently transpired. This fulfillment, as Matthew understood it, was accomplished when gentiles, having heard and accepted the gospel, joined with Israel in the worship of God (4:15-16; 8:11-13; 12:17-21). Christians challenged forms of behavior, such as the observance of dietary and sabbath laws, that for centuries had been essential marks of Jewish life. They accorded to Jesus, as Son of God, an authority higher than that of the law and the temple, a sure sign of blasphemy. They were traitors to Israel, because they had refused to join the desperate struggle for national independence in the war of A.D. 66 to 70. Into the intimacy of their homes and covenant meals they accepted "harlots," "tax collectors," "Gentiles." Their defense of such behavior attracted blunt rejection by synagogue leaders. Small wonder that a document addressed to a community so alienated from its neighbors should contain so many echoes of this hostility (e.g., 5:10-12; 10:16-33; 13:20-21; 20:1-19; 21:33-45; 23:13-39).

Where was such a church located? Probably in cities that had many Jewish synagogues and also a large gentile population, where the church had drawn members largely from the synagogues but also where there were numerous gentile members, and where there continued to be an active effort to convert both groups. We may infer from the fact the Gospel was written in Greek that the churches spoke Greek and used a Greek translation of the Old Testament (the Septuagint). It was a region where the Christian movement was rapidly growing in numbers and in strength, a growth that fueled Jewish resentments and gentile suspicions. Given these specifications, some scholars favor Palestine (A. Wikenhauser, T.H. Robinson), some Phoenicia (G.D. Kilpatrick), and some Syria (B.W. Bacon, F.V. Filson, G. Strecker). Those who ask for a particular city usually select Antioch-on-the-Orontes, the major seaport of ancient Syria (A.H. McNeile, B.H. Streeter, D.M. Smith, R.A. Spivey). For our purposes it is enough to select the region extending from northern Palestine through Syria.

I stress the fact that the audience was restricted to the churches of this region. In modern times almost all books are aimed at a general public, "to whom it may concern." In Matthew's day this was not true; books belonged to specific communities, and his was meant for believers only. He could therefore introduce many characters (John the Baptist, the Pharisees, Pilate) without identifying them and many ideas (the "kingdom of heaven," the "Son of man") without defining them. He did not need to prove to his readers that Jesus was Messiah, for his audience had already made this elementary confession. Had he been addressing an uncommitted or uninstructed public he would have written a different book.

I think he had in mind an even smaller audience, one composed mainly of *leaders* in the local churches. Their needs for *written* materials were far more numerous and constant than the needs of members in general. For their work a collection of the stories and sayings of Jesus would prove most useful. In many respects the church had adopted patterns of organization that had proved serviceable to the synagogues. During the first century these patterns had given a central role to the scribes.* Their power stemmed chiefly from their knowledge of the scriptures, their acquaintance with traditional interpretation, and their facility in counseling and

*Cf. Joachim Jeremias, *Jerusalem in the Time of Jesus* (Philadelphia: Fortress Press, 1969), pp. 233-45.

teaching people how to obey the revealed will of God. They had studied many years under the tutelage of renowned scholars until they had qualified for the revered title rabbi. They had earned the right to interpret the rules on matters of ritual, moral conduct, and civil and criminal justice. As teachers of the Torah they were the heirs of Moses' authority (23:2) and were accorded "the place of honor at feasts and the best seats in the synagogues [23:6]." They set the pattern for the faithful to follow in such practices as praying, almsgiving, and fasting (6:1-18). They exercised the power to bind or to loose, to assure members of entrance into the kingdom of heaven or to exclude them from it (16:19; 18:18; 23:13). On many disputed matters of faith or conduct the laity would first ask, "What do the scribes say?" (2:4; 17:10). And their answers, based on their knowledge of the written scriptures but given orally, carried great weight.

We visualize Matthew as such a scribal teacher, preparing a collection of the traditions for use by other Christian scribes as they carried on their professional work of oral instruction in the churches of the region. In Jesus' last instructions to the twelve he announced his intention to send out "prophets and wise men and scribes" to continue his battle with the Pharisaic scribes (23:34). This implies that the twelve and their successors, as Christian scribes, were to be received as accredited delegates of Jesus; their work was to be accepted as fully in line with that of the prophets. Matthew, then, prepared for scribal teachers and judges within the church a source book of the traditions of how Jesus—the master rabbi (23:8)—had communicated to his interns the mysteries and keys of the kingdom of heaven.*

In Matthew's eyes, there was a definite correlation between three groups mentioned in the Gospel and similar groups within the churches of his day. The first group consisted of the disciples, who were present in virtually all the scenes from their first summons until their last. We must

*Cf. M. Jack Suggs, *Wisdom, Christology, and Law in Matthew's Gospel* (Cambridge, MA: Harvard University Press, 1970), pp. 120-26.

remember that Matthew normally applied the term disciple to the twelve only, who were being trained for a special vocation, and not to all believers or followers. Disciples were required to leave their homes and former occupations to pursue an itinerant career with Jesus. They were granted special authority to preach, teach, and heal. Mysteries were explained to them that remained hidden to others. To them was promised a primary responsibility for occupying "twelve thrones, judging the twelve tribes of Israel [19:28]," a position comparable to the seat of Moses, on which the scribes of the Pharisees sat (23:2).

The second group, present in nearly every chapter of the book, were the crowds or multitudes. They were by no means as neutral or uncommitted as these words suggest. They were followers who hailed Jesus as prophet, who responded to his preaching, and who were healed at his command, forgiven by his assurance, and fed with food provided by his compassion. So convinced were they of his authority and so intent on worshiping him that the enemies of Jesus greatly feared them. Concern for them motivated much of Jesus' work with the twelve.

The third group, who furnished a constant foil for both story and teaching, were called most commonly "scribes and Pharisees." They were viewed as a "brood of vipers" from their first appearance (3:7f.) until their final effort to disprove the resurrection of Jesus (27:62). To be sure, the cast of villains shifts somewhat. Occasional mention is made of other groups— Sadducees, high priests, Herodians, and elders—but the Pharisees remain the most deadly antagonists. It is assumed that almost all unbelieving scribes belonged to the Pharisaic party and that, where other groups appeared, the Pharisees remained the core of opposition to Jesus, the twelve, and the crowds.

How, then, are these three groups correlated in Matthew's mind with the situation in his day? The twelve disciples correspond to the prophets, wise men, and scribes who were leaders in the churches of the second generation. The crowds of followers match the lay members of these churches. In bitter conflict with both these groups are the Pharisaic leaders of the rival synagogues. Thus, the audiences of Jesus are seen to correspond to the audiences of Matthew. When Matthew describes how Jesus trained the twelve to meet the needs of the crowds, he was concerned with providing help to his own colleagues in their care for the "little ones" as they faced their adversaries in the synagogues.

An analogy may be drawn from the practice in modern television of using a split screen so viewers can see two different locations simultaneously. For example, using videotape, a station can telecast a picture of President John Kennedy addressing a New York audience in 1961, while on the same screen an audience in Texas can see and hear another President addressing a rally in Wyoming. The instant comparison of the two sides of the screen presumably increases the knowledge and affects the attitudes of the Texas audience. Similarly, readers of Matthew, if they are sufficiently perceptive, can simultaneously hear the words of Jesus addressed initially to disciples, crowds, or Pharisees; the message of Matthew addressed to leaders or followers in the churches of Syria; and a segment of scripture designed to be heard by Christians today in Chicago. Most readers are accustomed, in listening to Matthew, to focusing their attention either on the first or on the third of these lines of communication. Throughout the chapters that follow I will help you listen in on the second line. To this end we look next at clues provided by Matthew's editorial work.

The Arrangement

Matthew's arrangement of the teachings of Jesus is quite different from that in the other Gospels. In Matthew these teachings are organized into five major "sermons," all concluded by a similar formula: "And when Jesus finished these sayings..." (7:28; 11:1; 13:53; 19:1; 26:1). This formula, along with the organization of each sermon, seems to be the editor's choice. I shall call these sermons "manuals" and explore the character of each in the light of Matthew's audience and its function in his story as a whole.

1. *A manual for church members* (4:23—7:28). Christian scribes served the churches as catechists, making clear to converts the basic requirements of the kingdom. Duties were formulated in brief, memorable teachings that the scribes conveyed on the authority of Jesus. Matthew served as a link between these scribes and their predecessors, the disciples of Jesus, by arranging what later came to be called the Sermon on the Mount. This sermon made clear who would inherit the kingdom (5:3-10), the behavior required to fulfill the new law (5:17-48), the motives that should mark their religious practices (6:1-18), and the obligations of those who wished to build their houses on the rock (6:19—7:27).

At the beginning and the end of this sermon two groups are distinguished and yet viewed simultaneously, even though this makes for awkwardness in setting the stage. At the outset the disciples are separated from the crowds, but at the end the crowds hail the teaching as carrying authority for them. In advance of the Sermon the editor has described the calling of disciples and the attraction of crowds of followers. It was the sight of these crowds and concern for their needs that compelled Jesus to give these teachings to his disciples for their use as future teachers of such crowds. Readers are therefore right in assuming that the manual applies to all who would enter the narrow gate, even though the central accent often falls on the special duties of teachers. As successors to the prophets, those teachers would be persecuted on his account (5:11f.). (In 5:11 the shift from third to second person may mark a shift of focus from the crowds to the disciples.) Their task is so to teach and obey Jesus' commands as to demonstrate their superiority to the Pharisaic scribes (5:19) and to raise the level of obedience on the part of the crowds. (Keep in mind throughout the commentary the rough equations I have mentioned: disciples = leaders in Matthew's churches; crowds = the membership of these churches; Pharisees = their opponents, the leaders of the synagogues.)

2. *A manual for physicians* (9:35—11:1). In this second
block of teachings it is easier to separate the two audiences.
Like the first, this manual was placed within the context of
Jesus' teaching, preaching, and healing in "all the cities and
villages" (9:35; 11:1). As in the first block, concern for the
crowds of followers prompted Jesus to turn to the disciples.
Unlike the first, this address was confined to these twelve,
dealing with tasks peculiar to them, tasks that linked their
work to what Jesus had been doing: healing, proclaiming,
teaching. Acting under powers delegated by him, they were
to proclaim the same news to the same cities. Their identification with him would become so complete that hospitality
accorded them would count as hospitality to him (cp. 25:31-
46).

Little doubt remains that in this sermon Matthew had in
mind the itinerant prophets and healers of his day. It provided
authorization and motivation for their travels, suggestions on
how to meet adversity, and assurances concerning the outcome of their work. With the slightest imagination one can
see in this chapter colorful snapshots of scribal missionaries
during the period when churches were dependent on them
and when these leaders faced precisely the dilemmas outlined
here.

A recent sociological study of the Jewish-Christian churches
of the first generation stresses the importance of the same
three groups: the revealer of divine secrets who has been
accepted as a redeemer, the group of itinerant charismatics
functioning as his spokespersons, the communes of those who
extend hospitality to those charismatics and who follow their
guidance.*

3. *A manual of kingdom secrets* (13:1-52). When Matthew
edited this collection of parables, he found it more difficult
to deal with his double audience, to distinguish yet not separate the two groups. Apparently, the parables belonged to

*Gerd Theissen, *Sociology of Early Palestinian Christianity* (Philadelphia: Fortress Press, 1978).

the crowds as the primary and ultimate audience of both Jesus and Matthew (13:1-9, 24-35). However, in at least some of the parables, knowledge of the hidden implications belonged only to the disciples. Their eyes and ears were blessed with understandings of divine secrets that had been denied other believers (13:11, 14-17). With this knowledge, "hidden since the foundation of the world [13:35]," they could recognize ways in which Satan obstructed their work (13:19-22) without losing confidence in a final victory. Their knowledge of the final judgment was needed in their work as judges (13:36-43), enabling them to serve as efficient "householders," providing whatever the household might need (13:52; cp. 24:45-51). In making these teachings accessible to the scribes of his day, Matthew was continuing this education in the secrets of the kingdom that Jesus had begun. Always in the background was Jesus' concern for the churches, the great crowds referred to in 13:2. They represented the soils on which the seed fell (13:4-8), or the field in which both wheat and weeds grew (13:24-30), or the net that caught both edible and inedible fish (13:47-50).

4. *A manual of discipline* (18:1—19:2). The scribes in the churches, like the Pharisees in the synagogues, exercised inescapable responsibilities in the field of discipline. It was right that they be warned, as in chapter 13, not to weed their field before the final harvest. But they could not avoid altogether the tasks of deciding delicate issues in the interim. For better or worse, they had been entrusted with the power to bind or to loose; this collection of sayings teaches them how to wield this power. They must be alert to the poisons of their profession: the tendency to judge people in terms of their social standing (18:1-5), to underestimate the degree to which their own policies might endanger their followers (18:7-9), to despise those less gifted than themselves (18:10-14), or to be too impatient with troublesome brothers (18:21-23). Like all rulers, they were prone to apply penalties too quickly, too publicly, and too harshly, forgetting the unlimited mercy with which God had treated the judges themselves (18:15-35). Such

methods of governing were threatened with final condemnation at the hands of their own King. In this collection of teachings the problems in Matthew's own churches come most clearly to the surface.

5. *A manual of signs* (24:1—26:1). Like the preceding sermon, this one was addressed to the disciples in private. It was introduced by a prophecy of the destruction of the temple (24:1-2) and by direct declarations that the Pharisees and scribes had defaulted on their obligations to help people enter the kingdom (23:13f.). The disciples of Jesus had inherited this same vocation (cp. 21:41); therefore, the closing address was designed to instruct them with regard to the coming of the kingdom and the best ways to prepare for it. The sermon began with pointed questions on which churches expected answers from their scribes: "What will be the sign of your coming and of the close of the age? [24:3]." Leaders were providing conflicting answers, a fact that tended to diminish confidence, to inflame fears, and to produce demoralization (24:9-12). The problem of how to distinguish false prophets from true had become especially acute (24:24), in view of the fact that Jesus had explicitly disavowed knowledge of the exact day and had been content to leave his disciples with the tantalizing command to watch (24:42). To Matthew, the best attitude toward signs of Christ's return was provided by a series of four parables that told what an absent lord expected of his servants (24:45—25:46). Those who defaulted on their assignments would merit eviction to the outer darkness as hypocrites, an epithet used elsewhere for Pharisaic scribes (24:51). Christ demanded that his scribes stay awake, and the only way to stay awake was to care continually for fellow servants (24:48). This kind of crisis demanded not diviners, but deacons.

Modern scholars largely agree in stressing the importance of these five manuals and in attributing their organization to Matthew. They do not agree on how the other sections of the Gospel, composed chiefly of stories, should be related to these five. If we are to grasp the basic structure of the Gospel, we

16

must examine these sections. How do they prepare for the five sermons? How do they set forth the developing relations between Jesus and his three chief audiences? What are the implications for Matthew's audiences?

At the beginning of the Gospel, Matthew incorporated three separate traditions about the origin of Jesus that he felt Christian scribes should know: (1) the book of genealogy, (2) the story of conception, (3) the story of the flight from Judea to Egypt and then to Galilee. I shall comment on these in due course. In form, function, and content they are quite distinct from what we might call Book One, 3:1—7:28.

Chapters 3:1—4:22 function as a necessary introduction to the first manual as well as to all later sections of the Gospel. The same three groups hold the center of the stage. John's announcement of the kingdom, with the command to repent, attracted the crowds who continued to follow Jesus throughout the Gospel (3:1-6; 4:23-25). The same prophetic message attracted hostility from the Pharisees and Sadducees, who are castigated as a brood of vipers (3:7). They provide a foil for John's message as well as for several teachings of Jesus' opening sermon. Third in order, the disciples are introduced in the person of four fishermen who leave their nets on the promise of being taught how to fish for people (4:18-22). The Sermon on the Mount constitutes the first lesson.

Three chapters are assigned to Book Two of Matthew's design: 8:1—10:42. Nowhere in the entire Gospel do the crowds figure more constantly than in chapters 8 and 9, where they provide an occasion for Jesus to send workers into the harvest field (9:38). In these two chapters there is a long cycle of healing stories that focus attention on the crowds who followed Jesus because they recognized his authority (8:1). These stories show how he "took *our* infirmities and bore *our* diseases [8:17]." The use of the first person plural reflects Matthew's stance. He identified himself with crowds who had been sick, who had come to Jesus and had been healed. To Matthew, each cure was a sign of the powerful presence of the kingdom, which was made known primarily in the exercise of God's mercy (8:29; 9:6, 13, 35; 11:4-5). He did not overlook the fact that one member of the crowd was a Roman centurion whose faith was stronger than could be found in Israel. The cure of the centurion's servant by this physician was seen by Matthew as creating an important precedent (8:5-13).

This cycle of stories seems to be saying, "Are you unable to see the signs that God's kingdom has begun to dawn? Look at members of these crowds whose faith brought healing to them. Their blindness has been healed so that they can vouch for the new day" (9:27-31).

Although the dominant accent in Book Two falls on the healing of the crowds, a secondary accent falls on the training of Jesus' scribes. Each scribe was called to lead a homeless existence in which the new duties, as outlined in chapter 10, took priority over the usual obligations to parents (8:18-22). Because social hostility was the inevitable consequence of such training, the scribe needed to become immunized to fears of death (8:23-27) and to accept without hesitation the guilt-by-association with outcasts (9:9-13). All this was incumbent on these future "shepherds" (9:36).

Set against the scribes who followed Jesus were the scribes who cried blasphemy (cp. 8:19; 9:3). Cures that impelled the crowds to glorify God aroused the scribes' anger; they complained that such cures were due to Jesus' use of the devil's powers (9:34). As the gentile soldier represented the faith of the crowds, so these scribes represented those "sons of the kingdom" who would be cast into "outer darkness" (8:11-13). Jesus guaranteed that his interns would incur hostility from this same source (10:25).

To introduce Book Three and to prepare for the manual of kingdom secrets in chapter 13, the editor showed how hostility against Jesus would steadily become more acute (11:1—12:50). Successive acts of mercy only provoked more bitter accusations (12:2, 10, 24). It was now obvious that "this generation" had already rejected the message of both John and Jesus (11:18-19); Jesus responded by harsh words, condemning recalcitrant cities (11:20-24). By contrast, the crowds were pictured as the blind, the lame, the leprous, the deaf, the poor, and even the dead, who had accepted God's invitation, first from John and then from Jesus (11:4-6). They could be described as a company of babes to whom secrets had been revealed that had been hidden from the wise. They were seen as meek and burdened folk who had begun to carry the Messiah's gentle and easy yoke (11:25-30). It was to them that Jesus told the parables of chapter 13, making clear how the true heirs of the kingdom would become the target of Satan's deceptions. Jesus turned the conflicts with the Pharisees into occasions for instructing his disciples on the nature of the sabaath (12:1-14), on how to discern the strategies of the devil, and how to respond to the demand for signs (12:22-42). Even more strikingly, Jesus identified his family as the company of those who, by dint of obeying God's call, had become his brothers and sisters (12:46-50). All this is how the editor prepared the way for the series of parables that described the varying responses to Jesus' message and that helped the disciples understand these responses. Such is the central function of Book Three: 11:1—13:52.

Now to the shape of Book Four. As noted earlier, chapter 18 deals with the problems of church discipline. In the preceding chapters (13:53—17:27) Matthew shows a special interest in how Jesus trained the twelve to care for the crowds. Twice this training had involved lessons on how to feed them. In both cases (14:13-21; 15:32-39) the story stressed the initial incompetence of the disciples, followed by their ability, after Jesus had blessed the food (14:19; 15:36), to feed thousands. In an epilogue this incident was made the occasion for private instruction concerning the "leaven of the Pharisees" (16:5-12). These chapters also deal with how the training of apprentices included the ability to heal the sick. When the twelve failed to provide a cure, their master rebuked them for their lack of faith, and he himself did what was as yet impossible for them (17:14-21). When Jesus wanted to know the mind of the crowd concerning himself, he asked the disciples; the answers to this poll showed the crowd believed that Jesus, like earlier prophets, was exercising the authority of God (16:13f.).

This section of the Gospel clarified the qualifications that would be necessary if the twelve were to serve the crowds after

Jesus' death. Conversations near Caesarea Philippi showed how their future work required three things: a recognition of Jesus as Son of God, an understanding of why Jesus' mission required his death, and a readiness to accept their own death for his sake (16:13-28). Of these three requirements, only the first was as yet realized. So we see Book Four as part of the process of inducting scribes into the mysteries of the kingdom, preparing them not only to understand the Passion of Jesus, but even more to undertake their later work in feeding, healing, and governing his flock.

In Book Five—where the scene shifts from Galilee to Judea, the stronghold of the Pharisees (19:1-3)—Matthew arranged his materials in such a way as to dramatize the mounting conflict between Jesus and his enemies. This section includes a series of debates between Jesus and the leaders of the synagogues, materials that had been widely used before Matthew's day by Christian teachers (19:3-9; 21:23-37; 22:15-46). The debates prompted a series of parables in which the Pharisees "perceived that he was speaking about them" (21:28—22:10). The battles reached a verbal climax in the seven woes against the "scribes and Pharisees" (23:13-39).

These parables and woes may have been launched originally in direct confrontation with the enemies; Matthew, however, was primarily concerned with using them in the instruction of his own churches—leaders and followers. The conflict over divorce, for example, introduced a saying about sacrifices yet to be made by the disciples (19:10-12). So, also, the interchange with the rich man became an assurance of reward for these sacrifices (19:23-30). The woes against Jesus' enemies became an occasion for urging the crowds to observe whatever the Pharisees had commanded, all the while the disciples were commanded to shun the pompous hypocrisies of their predecessors (23:1-12). In fact, the surly opposition of synagogue leaders proved to be counterproductive. Dangers only increased the spontaneous enthusiasm of the crowds who had followed Jesus from Galilee to Judea (21:1-11). In turn, the hosannas of these worshiping "children" had only aggravated the animosities of the leaders (21:14-16). So these chapters served to clarify for Matthew's readers the opposing and interacting roles of disciples, crowds, and Pharisees, as the death of Jesus came nearer.

These roles were most transparently described in two of the parables Jesus addressed to the synagogue leaders and that represent, in miniature, the whole Gospel. According to the first (21:33-46), God, as owner, had leased a vineyard (Israel) to a first set of tenants. These tenants had refused to pay the owner's portion of the harvest and had killed the owner's son in order to claim the vineyard for themselves. Nothing was left but to evict and kill these tenants (the unrepentant leaders of Israel) and to let the vineyard out to new tenants (the disciples) who would give the owner the proper share of the harvest. The crowds, whom the Pharisees had feared and who had held Jesus to be a prophet, represented both the vineyard and the harvest that belonged to God. The parable thus covered the whole complex web of relationships that had existed between Jesus and his enemies, his crowd and his disciples; at the same time the parable illuminated a similar alignment of forces in the Evangelist's own time.

In the story of the wedding feast (22:1-14) Matthew's concern for his churches became more obvious. Only the first stage of the story dealt with the situation in Jesus' day, when invitations to the feast had been spurned by those invited (the Pharisees). Matthew was more interested in the second stage, after guests had arrived in the banqueting hall (i.e., the crowds of believing Jews and gentiles, harlots and publicans). Some of these guests (i.e., members of Matthew's churches; cp. 13:36-43) were in danger of being cast into the outer darkness. The previous fate of the Pharisees now threatened Christians, unless they learned the lessons of chapter 23 and unless they rightly discerned the signs of the times, as taught by the parables of chapters 24 and 25. Thus Book Five.

Obviously, the Gospel would be incomplete without the last three chapters (26—28). The author has in fact been preparing for them from the very beginning (Herod's fear of this king in chapter 2 is perhaps the earliest omen of the crucifixion). In these chapters Matthew depicted the apparent success of the murderous efforts of Jesus' enemies (23:3ff.), but he also gave a final lesson in the training of the disciples. This lesson prevented them from forgetting either their own treachery (26:35, 56) or their final appointment (28:16-20). The last meal with Jesus had marked the sealing of a covenant which underscored both the treachery and the appointment (26:20-29). We may note that in Book Five one of the groups which had been present in earlier episodes seems to be strikingly absent: the crowds of followers (not to be confused with the crowds that "followed" the synagogue rulers—26:47, 55; 27:15, 20). To be sure, the women, whose word to the disciples from the empty tomb proved so decisive, represented these followers (27:55; 28:1-10). Yet Matthew appears to have believed that the crowds who followed Jesus had been scattered (26:31), and that they would be gathered again only through the work of the disciples in Galilee after a final mandate had been issued to them by the risen Lord. The last three chapters were a preparation for this final mandate.

Summarizing this analysis of how the editor arranged his materials, then, we see the Gospel is divided into seven major sections:

Traditions concerning the origin of Jesus
    The book of genealogy (1:1-17)
    The story of the conception (1:18-25)
    Travels from Judea to Egypt and to Galilee (2:1-23)
Book One—Beginnings in the work of salvation
    The work of John (3:1-12)
    The work of Jesus (3:13—4:22)
    A manual for church members (4:23—7:29)
Book Two—The physician and the crowds
    Cases of therapy (8:1—9:34)
    A manual for physicians (9:35—11:1)
Book Three—The mysterious presence of the kingdom
    Separation of the violent from the gentle (11:2—12:50)
    A manual of kingdom secrets (13:1-52)
Book Four—The care of the crowds
    Training disciples to feed them (13:53—16:12)

Revealing the keys to messianic power (16:13—17:27)
A manual of discipline (18:1—19:2)
Book Five—Preparation for the Passion
The reversal of status (19:3—20:28)
The messianic demonstration (20:29—21:22)
Confrontation in the temple (21:23—24:2)
A manual of signs (24:3—25:46)
Covenant and mandate (26:1—28:20)
The Passover covenant (26:1-56)
Trial and denial (26:57—27:10)
Crucifixion of a king (27:11-54)
Final mandate (27:55—28:20)

Date

Establishing the character of the churches and the types of problems they faced is of greater importance than determining the year of the Gospel's publication. In fact, the nature of these problems is the best index of the publication date. The document must have appeared after the conflicts between church and synagogue had reached maximum intensity and perhaps after the synagogues had initiated the practice of expelling followers of Jesus, but before the church had broken off contact with the synagogues or had ceased an active mission to Israel. The debate of scholars over the date depends partly on their reading of the evidence concerning these church-synagogue relationships. To what extent had the church parted company with the Jewish community? Or had it continued to exist as a cluster of synagogues, obliged to recognize the authority of the scribes (23:2) and to pay the temple tax (17:27)?

Answers to such questions do not enable us to fix on a narrow span of years. Consequently, some scholars wisely adopt a broad span of time, between A.D. 70 and 110 (Stendahl, Davies, MacKenzie, Wikenhauser). The year 70 is chosen because of the probability that Matthew knew and used Mark, a document that had not appeared before A.D. 64 at the earliest, and because he referred to the destruction of Jerusalem in the war of A.D. 66 to 70 (Matthew 21:41; 22:7; 23:36; 24:15, although no one is certain these texts refer to this event). The year 110 is chosen because of the likelihood that Ignatius of Antioch was acquainted with Matthew (one should compare the following texts: Polycarp 2:2—Matthew 10:16; Smyrnaeans 1:1—Matt. 3:15; Smyr. 6:1—Matt. 19:12; Trallians 11:1—Matt. 15:13; Ephesians 5:2—Matt 18:19; Eph. 6:1—Matt. 10:40; Eph. 7:1—Matt. 7:6; Eph. 14:2—Matt. 12:33). I find it wiser to accept this forty-year period than to argue for a narrower span, as suggested by other scholars: A.D. 80 to 90, by Streeter and Goodspeed; A.D. 90 to 100, by Bacon, Kilpatrick, and Strecker; A.D. 80 to 100, by Bonnard and Filson. That a considerable period had elapsed since the days of Jesus is implied by the phrase "to this day" (27:8; 28:15).

Sources

To recover the precise extent and form of the materials Matthew incorporated within his Gospel is no easy matter; many of these materials would have been discarded after he used them. Even so, the business of interpretation requires some conjecture about these sources. I suppose, along with most other exegetes, that Matthew himself created few of the episodes in his narrative; rather, he was a collector of stories and teachings already in circulation. The first generation of Christians had, no doubt, preserved the memories of Jesus in various ways. There had been apostles who had cherished and recounted their own recollections. Members of the crowds in Galilee had presumably become members of the earliest house-churches and had shared with one another their vivid memories of Jesus. Three other types of material probably circulated from a very early period:

- oral accounts of the ministry, passion, and resurrection that formed the basis of sermons preached by missionaries to the unconverted (e.g., Acts 10:36-43)

- oral summaries of the parables and commands of Christ that formed the basis of catechetical instruction of converts (e.g., 1 Peter 1:13—3:12)
- passages from scripture that, when read in the light of the traditions about Jesus, showed how God had fulfilled the "promises given to the patriarchs" (Romans 15:8)

In all probability, separate collections of these materials had appeared in written form before the date of Matthew. Near the end of the first generation an edition containing many of these materials had appeared in the Gospel of Mark, which was, so far as we know, the earliest connected account of the ministry of Jesus and the training of the apostles.

By the second generation the supply of personal memories had ceased to grow. Matthew appears to have been totally dependent on materials—oral or written—provided by others than eyewitnesses. About half his Gospel runs parallel to the narrative materials of Mark. Did Mark use Matthew or did Matthew use Mark? For a century the predominant vote of scholars has been for the latter alternative, and with this vote I concur. For almost all his narratives Matthew bases his record on that of Mark and omits only a few of the stories he found in Mark's Gospel (e.g., Mark 1:23-28; 7:32-37; 8:22-26; 9:38-40; 12:41-44).

In several large sections Matthew also adopts the order in which the Marcan narratives appear (e.g., Matthew 3 and 4, but especially chapters 14 to 27). Usually, plausible reasons can be given for Matthew's occasional alteration of the order and for his omission or addition of various details. His editorial "habit" led him to abbreviate many narratives and to expand the didactic discourses. He liked to add Old Testament passages whose fulfillment he detected (Matthew 21:2-5; 26:15; 27:9-10; 27:34). At times his changes in Mark seem to reflect different conceptions of Christ, different attitudes toward the twelve, or different pedagogic standards (19:9). The study of all these changes has become the basic starting point for efforts to reconstruct the editorial perspectives of Matthew.*

In about 200 verses the material in Matthew deviates from Mark and reflects a similarity to Luke. These verses deal mainly with sayings attributed to Jesus. In some cases the degree of coincidence is extensive (Matthew 6:22-34; 7:3-5; 23:37-39). In one passage, for example, twenty-four identical Greek words appear in the same order (Matthew 7:7,8; Luke 11:9, 10). In other areas variation in wording or in order is so great as to force the student to doubt a common source (e.g., Matthew 5:1-48; 7:13-27; 10:26-39). Even where Matthew and Luke reflect a common origin the striking contrasts in order often leave us uncertain whether or not this common origin was a single, firmly structured written source. With many other scholars, I posit the existence of a cycle of sayings that both Matthew and Luke used, calling this cycle of teachings Q (for the German *Quelle*, meaning source); one cannot know with assurance, however, whether Q was a single source, whether it was written or oral, or whether it reached the two Evangelists with the same wording in the same order. To reconstruct Q's beginning, end, or internal structure is quite impossible.

Other traditions, now found only in Matthew, were probably in circulation before Matthew's Gospel appeared. For instance, a group of eleven passages link the events of the Gospel to scripture (1:22; 2:6, 15, 17, 23; 4:14; 8:17; 12:17; 13:35; 21:4; 27:9). These may have originated in Jewish-Christian circles and may have been used by apostles before Matthew. The attitude toward these prophecies is akin to that expressed by Paul in Romans 15:8-9: "Christ became a servant to the circumcised to show God's truthfulness, in order to confirm the promises given to the patriarchs, and in order that the Gentiles might glorify God for his mercy." This confirmation of God's promises to Israel is stressed in four of the eleven passages (1:22; 2:6, 15; 21:4); the glorification of God

*For summary, cf. J. Rohde, *Rediscovering the Teachings of the Evangelists* (London: SCM Press, 1968), pp. 47-112.

by the gentiles is stressed in three (4:14; 8:17; 12:17); in two passages God's desire for mercy is the point at issue (9:13; 12:7). Because this conception of promise and fulfillment is so characteristic of Matthew, it is unwise to insist that in these appeals to scripture he must have depended on a separate source. He may well have used such a source, but if so, the choice of specific citations at strategic spots in the narrative (e.g., 4:14; 12:17) was his.

Another instance of pre-Matthean material is the collection of stories concerning Jesus' lineage (1:1-17), his conception (1:18-25), and his infancy (2:1-23). As we shall see, the motivation and use of these stories was distinct from Matthew's own purposes; accordingly, they seem to reflect marks of independent origin.

How does one account for the origin of ten parables found only in Matthew? We may well doubt that Matthew created all these stories. In form they reflect the processes of oral rather than written tradition. Parables told orally tended to gravitate into cycles; after a time these cycles were written down by teachers. In all likelihood this latter step had been taken earlier than the date of the Gospel. Most of these parables are introduced by formulas common to rabbinic literature. Some of them fulfill the function of training scribes in the nature of the kingdom of heaven (13:44-52); some deal with problems of church discipline as faced by scribes (13:24-30, 36-43; 18:23-35); some with the debates with leaders of the synagogues (21:1-16, 28-32; 22:1-14); some with the question of how church leaders could best prepare for the coming of the Son of man (25:1-46). They embody traditions that had long been useful in the churches—traditions saturated with Jewish-Christian ethos, oriented toward continuing debates with the synagogue and the special duties of church leaders. It was these features, no doubt, that commended these parabolic materials—whether oral or written—to Matthew.

Possibly, still other materials in the Gospel came to the editor in organized oral or written form, but to recover this form is extremely difficult. For example, there may have been a series of seven woes against the scribes and Pharisees (23:13-

36). Even more probable, a neatly organized triad of instructions on almsgiving, prayer, and fasting (6:1-6, 16-18) may have been linked to yet another triad, the three antitheses concerning anger, lust, and deceit (5:21-22, 27-28, 33-34a, 37). If a single written document existed that contained teaching peculiar to Matthew (which some scholars call M), these two triads may well have provided its core.

Some students of Matthew want to press farther the exploration of these earlier sources, desiring to probe to the origins of the Matthew traditions, whether in the period intervening between Jesus' death and the composition of Matthew, or in the days of Jesus' own ministry. These students will find it necessary to consult a synopsis of the first three Gospels. For this purpose I recommend *Gospel Parallels* (New York: Thomas Nelson, 1949). For tracing the successive changes made by Matthew in the sources as they came to him I recommend F.W. Beare, *The Earliest Records of Jesus* (Nashville: Abingdon Press, 1962).

A study of Matthew, however, does not require a detailed study of the origins of each paragraph in the Gospel. It is perhaps more important to understand the final form of this Gospel and its use in teaching local congregations. For this purpose I recommend a concentration on the *Revised Standard Version* of the Gospel. To supplement my own commentary, I have appended a bibliography of scholarly studies, limited to books readily available in English to pastors and teachers in local congregations.

Chapter II

~~~

TRADITIONS CONCERNING
THE ORIGIN OF JESUS

The Book of Genealogy (1:1-17)

When wise men from the East came seeking the king of
the Jews, King Herod was impelled to consult the scribes (2:1-
6), whose duty it was not only to interpret the scriptures, but
also to keep the annals of the national history. Similar duties
fell on the Christian scribes, to whom we owe the development
and preservation of this "book of the genealogy."* By the
second generation (A.D. 60-90) there were at least two such
lists: Matthew gives us one; Luke, (3:23-38) the other.

What were the chief motives at work in the production
of such genealogies? Modern studies have overstressed the
desire to prove to unbelieving Jews that Jesus was the Messiah
because he was a son of Abraham and a son of David (1:1).
An apologetic appeal of this sort would have been uncon-
vincing. There were so many sons of Abraham in Jesus' day
that a list like this one would hardly prove he alone was the
Messiah. Christians among whom these lists circulated had
already accepted him on much more persuasive grounds. A
more compelling motive was the wish to affirm that in sending
Jesus to govern God's people Israel (2:6), God had vindicated
the faith of the fathers. God had confirmed the promises he
had made to Abraham, to David, and to the prophets of the
Exile. "The great patriarchs who stand at the beginning of
Jewish history will also have an important role at its comple-

---

*M.D. Johnson, *The Purpose of the Biblical Genealogies* (New York:
Cambridge University Press, 1969), pp. 139-228.

tion."* To each generation these promises had been extended; now each generation participated in the salvation that had come (Matthew 8:11; cp. Hebrews 11:1-40). In recalling the promises made to these fathers, the church confessed its solidarity with all generations since Adam, with forgotten men like Ram and Azor, as well as with famous men like Isaac and Solomon.

The organization of the list around three pivotal points suggests other convictions. As "son of Abraham," the Messiah represented the fulfillment of racial solidarity, the covenant of circumcision that signaled the patriarch's faith in God's promise (cp. Romans 4). As "son of David," the Messiah's work was continuous with the political and national hopes of David, the first king. The kingdom of heaven ruled by this king fulfilled promises made to David. Just as all past frustration in the history of Israel has been symbolized by the deportation to Babylon, so the events celebrated by the church marked the true liberation. The genealogies document the conviction that it was the mainstream of Israel's history which had reached its goal in Jesus (e.g., the reference to all twelve sons of Jacob in 1:2).

Another motive may be seen in the appearance of five women: Tamar, Rahab, Ruth, Uriah's wife, and Mary. The inclusion of women in a genealogy that, in a culture dominated by males, usually listed only "the fathers" is surprising. Some of these women were non-Jewish, and by the standards of the Torah, some had been notorious sinners. Yet, however humble or despised, they had been significant instruments through whom God had kept covenant with the people, maintaining them in existence from the beginning. Their presence provided impressive precedent for including gentiles and harlots within the church and for defending its polyglot membership as an authentic fulfillment of earlier tendencies. Linking Mary to these other women may also have been one way of meeting attacks on her chastity and her son's legitimacy (1:19). (For the traditional stories of these women, cf. Tamar,

*Ibid, p. 219

Genesis 38; Rahab, Joshua 2; Ruth, Ruth 4:13-22; Uriah's wife, 2 Samuel 11.)

Matthew probably had a good reason for organizing the genealogy into three sections of fourteen generations each, although his precise reason is difficult to recapture. Numbers are helpful in memorization. Jewish oral traditions made much of the numbers two, three, and seven. But three series of fourteen are not often encountered. Were readers expected to figure that forty-two equals six weeks of seven days each, bringing Israel at the birth of Christ to the opening of the seventh week, the sabbatical rest of the kingdom of God? Or were readers expected to associate forty-two with the forty-two months that equaled three and a half years, which, in certain types of apocalyptic numerology, represented the time of Israel's waiting for the fulfillment of God's promise? (See, e.g., Revelation 11:2.) Our knowledge of the symbolism of numbers is not adequate to recapture the original connotations.

Even though much is obscure we may be confident that, to Jewish Christians, the genealogy would have been a welcome way of accenting their continuity with the life of Israel from the beginning, whereas to gentile Christians it would have suggested an important element in their identity as brothers and sisters of the Messiah. It would have conveyed to them a clear idea of what their Jewish brothers meant when they spoke of Jesus as "the Messiah," i.e., "the Christ." It also would explain why their Jewish-Christian teachers could think of them, although gentiles, as children of Abraham. Their faith demonstrated God's power to raise up from stones descendants of Abraham (3:9).

We can thus recover a number of the reasons why Matthew should have begun his Gospel with this genealogy. But we have not yet mentioned a glaring contradiction at the heart of the genealogy, a feature that seems to contradict these other values. On the one hand Jesus is linked to his ancestors through Joseph, yet on the other hand the story recognizes that Joseph was not the father of Jesus. This means the chain that connected Jesus to Abraham appears to be broken at its most important link. This is surely a strange way to argue that Jesus was the Messiah promised to Abraham, to David, and the exiles in Babylon. Was the Evangelist aware of this apparent break in the chain? As a converted Jewish scribe, familiar with the scriptures, he must have been. Why, then, did Matthew include the contradiction in his narrative, and even focus attention on it by tracing forty-two generations to Joseph and then by making the sudden shift to Jesus' mother instead of his father? An answer to this question is deferred to the end of this section.

The Story of the Conception (1:18-25)

Matthew probably designed his Gospel to serve as the *only* gospel for churches in his region; he therefore included all that he felt was significant enough to justify preservation in writing. In these verses we probably have the entire tradition about Jesus' birth, all of it that had come to Matthew. This tradition embraced three separate concerns:

1. In verse 18 we have what is doubtless the core of the story: the identity of the mother, the name of her husband, and the announcement that she had become pregnant through the Holy Spirit. These three convictions seem to have been widely shared by churches other than Matthew's; they formed the core of various traditions concerning Jesus' birth.

2. In the rest of the unit the story dealt with a difficulty which confronted the church the moment an announcement had been made that Jesus had been "conceived by the Holy Spirit." Adversaries could and did say, "If Jesus was not the son of Joseph, then Mary was an adulteress and Jesus a bastard child." We do not know how early this debate with the synagogue developed, but the story reflected one stage in this debate: it gave a Christian defense against the charges. According to this defense Joseph had from the first sensed how scandalous the situation was. He had wanted to fulfill the requirements of the law by securing a divorce, but this desire had been countermanded by angelic authority. The child had not been illegitimate at all but had come in direct fulfillment

of Isaiah's prophecy (Isaiah 7:14). Rather than destroying Christian faith, the apparent scandal had been essential to God's determination to "save his people from their sins [1:21]."

3. The third concern was to provide basic explanations of the names given to the child. These names had been conferred in response to divine command and in fulfillment of earlier prophecy. The very name *Jesus* symbolized his later work, which would be to "save his people from their sins [v. 21]." Was Mary a sinner? Was her son conceived in sin? Not at all. It was as savior from sins that he was conceived and named. And the object of this salvation: "*his* people," including those who, like Joseph, had at first been offended by the mode of his conception. The second name, *Emmanuel,* carried a similar cluster of meanings; negatively, it disproved charges of defying the scriptures; and positively, it expressed the conviction of God's presence: "Where Jesus is, there God is" (cf. 11:25-30; 18:20). The repetition of the motif of 1:23c in 28:20b indicates a significant conviction of the editor; it was his way of bracketing the whole story between this promise and its fulfillment.

Travels from Judea to Egypt and to Galilee (2:1-23)

That a single unit of tradition should be so long as this is unusual in the Gospels; yet the various episodes within it are so interlocked as to resist breaking them apart. The strongest emphasis falls on repeated occasions of God's providential protection of this child from his enemies. The greatest danger to him stemmed from the king—first from Herod, troubled by the birth of a competitor, and then from his successor, Archelaus (v. 22). (Herod the Great [37-4 B.C.], widely known as opposed to messianic movements within his territory, was succeeded in 4 B.C. by his three sons. One of these was Herod Antipas, tetrarch of Galilee and Peraea during the ministry of Jesus. Archelaus, the most brutal of the three, became ethnarch of Judea, Samaria, and Idumaea but created so much resentment among his subjects that in A.D. 6 he was summoned to Rome and exiled to Gaul.) One means for providing protection for the child was a series of four dreams in which God issued instructions, first to the wise men (v. 12) and then to Joseph (vv. 13, 19, 22). Other indications of divine guidance were provided by the star (vv. 2, 9),* and by the prophecies contained in scripture (vv. 5, 15, 17-18, 23).

The various actors gave their testimony, sometimes unwittingly, to the divine design. First came the Magi, priestly astrologers, who were impelled to "come to worship him." In their journey Matthew foresaw the pilgrimage of the gentiles into the worshiping church, the next clue to which appears in 4:15-16. Probably he also saw in their journey the fulfillment of the prophecy in Isaiah 60:3: "And nations shall come to your light, and kings to the brightness of your rising." The wealth they brought was a sign of this fulfillment (Isaiah 60:6; cf. also Revelation 21:24-26). By dramatic gesture these pilgrims proclaimed the advent of a new king of the Jews. So, too, did the chief priests and scribes with their selection of Bethlehem as the prophesied birthplace (vv. 4-6). So, too, did Herod by his pogrom against the infants in Ramah, fulfilling prophecy but failing his objective. The infancy story is, to some degree, a preview of the enmities that characterized the ministry of Jesus. The story shows the impotence of humans to prevent God from accomplishing God's purpose. To be sure, Jesus would in the end be killed but not until the promised salvation had been realized.

Theological symbolism may be found in several geographical references. The pilgrimage from the East by gentile wise men called to mind promises of kings streaming to Jerusalem with the wealth of nations (e.g., Isaiah 2:1-4; 43:5-10; 60:6-14). So, too, the flight of Joseph's family to Egypt and the return to Israel recalled the patriarchal sagas of an earlier enslavement and liberation. Matthew was writing for churches that found a symbolic significance in the choice of

---

*Cf. Jean Danielou, *Primitive Christian Symbols* (New York: Taplinger Publishing Co., Inc., 1963), pp. 102-23.

Galilee and Nazareth over Judea. Jerusalem would become the center of the most stubborn opposition (2:3 and chap. 22), whereas in Galilee, Jesus would receive the greatest support from the crowds (4:23-25). Thus the story of the infancy recalled places (the East, Israel, Egypt, Galilee) that evoked in Jewish memories the whole saga of God's earlier dealings with Israel. This story had probably developed within a Jewish-Christian community and had been shaped by its experience of hostility from national leaders and of hospitality from the common people, whether Jewish or gentile.

As we recall the incidents in these two opening chapters we may well ask two questions: Does any one feature run through all segments of the story? What significance did this feature hold for the Christian congregations to whom Matthew was writing?

One feature, often overlooked, seems to recur in at least ten places. We noticed in the genealogy the surprising mention of five women, some of whom were of dubious notoriety. We also noticed the surprising and illogical tracing of the generations to Joseph, followed by the acknowledgment that Jesus was not Joseph's son. Then there was the surprising development when Joseph learned of the pregnancy of his fiancée. And there was the message of the angel that this fetus, conceived under conditions that to all observers would have marked sin, would save his people from their sins. Instead of marking God's alienation from the people, the child would mark God's most sure presence among them. The story of the wise men has similar anomalies. The star guided them on their journey as far as Jerusalem, but there they became dependent on directions from Herod. Herod, when consulted, was dependent in turn on the priests and scribes, but his efforts to profit from their instructions were foiled. These same scribes, although they could predict the right place on the basis of scripture, took no action on the matter; their knowledge proved to be of no use to them. Even though born in Bethlehem according to the prophecy, the baby was really called out of Egypt. On the trip from Egypt, however, the itinerary was suddenly changed; first directed to go to Judea, Joseph, while en route, was assigned rather to Galilee. How, then, may we summarize the feature common to these stories?

At every step there is an element of surprise, of innovation, but there is also an element of a planned fulfillment. Expectations are in fact fulfilled, yet never in such a way as to enable participants to anticipate the place, the time, and the precise method of fulfillment. The law and the prophets are honored, yet often in a way to embarrass those who most relied on them. A continuity is established between the story of Israel as a whole and the story of Jesus as a whole; but this continuity, as human beings view it, is broken time and again by divine decision, so that what appear to be broken links preserve the chain's unity. Among these broken links are those that symbolize God's reactions to human, and especially to Jewish, opposition: Herod, the priests and scribes, Archelaus, Judea, and even Joseph until he obeys the angel's instructions. God's spontaneous actions, so surprising to the human personnel, seem always to be occasioned by resistance to God's overall design, so that there is a transcendent consistency in what otherwise appears to be inconsistent. In this respect these keynote chapters illustrate themes that recur later in the Gospel: "I have come not to abolish [the law and the prophets] but to fulfil them....Not an iota, not a dot, will pass from the law until all is accomplished [5:17-18]." Yet all fulfillments of the law take place in such a way that they seem to abolish the law. So much for an answer to the first question.

Why, then, should Matthew have stressed this aspect both of "the book of genealogy" and of "the birth of Jesus Christ"? Not to prove to his readers that Jesus was the Messiah, and not to provide childish legends to serve as the script for sentimental Christmas pageants! Did Matthew wish to remind adult readers that God always "moves in mysterious ways his wonders to perform"? To urge believers who were bearing the brunt of opposition from the synagogue not to break off the dangerous mission to Israel, because God had not done so in the first instance? To encourage missionaries who were inclined to despair of success by showing how God had earlier used "the wrath of men" as an opportunity for new advances? To locate at the outset of Jesus' story the precedent for the later emergence of a mission to gentiles and to show how it had been Jewish recalcitrance that had been at least partially the reason for the mission? To tell in story fashion how the coming of Jesus himself had been God's greatest miracle, and how all lesser miracles in his story had been simply ways of pointing to this one breakthrough into the regularities of human history and into the patterns of human logic and language? We cannot know the answers to such questions; we can only guess at the editor's motives for including these stories as appropriate prelude to the work of the adult Jesus. We can be confident, however, that the editor wanted to assure all Christian teachers that God had chosen to continue in Jesus the pattern of promises-and-surprises that had characterized God's presence with Israel since the days of Abraham, David, and the Exile.

Chapter III

~~~~~~~~

BEGINNINGS IN
THE WORK OF SALVATION

The Work of John (3:1-12)

In reading this story that opens with the public announcement of God's kingdom, we should ask what was the significance for Matthew and his readers of his beginning at this point. The question must be raised, because it was the habit of biblical people to find at the outset of a story a kind of preview of all that would follow. An inaugural episode was like a seed which carried within it all that would emerge as it germinated and grew toward its own fruition. In this case the episode foreshadowed not only the later mission of Jesus, but the mission of his followers as well.

Both Jesus and his followers traced back their mission to the word and work of a prophet, assigned by God to call to repentance all who listened. Their response—a confession of sins and a group baptism—represented a decisive break with the past and an entrance into a new epoch freed from the frustrations of sin. Symbolically, this transition was marked by a descent into water, by the descent from heaven of the Holy Spirit, and by the winnowing and purging effects of fire. What happened to them signaled God's determination to raise up children to Abraham, if need be from stones. This determination on God's part initiated the fateful struggle between the prophet, as God's agent, and the Pharisees and Sadducees, those leaders of Israel who had pledged themselves to God's service. In all these respects Matthew's readers could find in the story of John an authentic introduction to their own stories.

All this reflected on Matthew's part a high appraisal of John. He had been a prophet who had come as the fulfillment of Isaiah's promise. His style of life had linked him to Elijah (2 Kings 1:8), whose return had been awaited as a sign of the Great Day (Malachi 4:5; Matthew 11:14; 17:11-12). John had announced the approach of the same kingdom as had Jesus and had leveled the same demand for repentance (3:2; 4:17). John and Jesus had been welcomed by the same groups and had been rejected by the same enemies (3:5; 4:25; 11:7-19). Their two vocations had been so closely aligned that contemporaries had easily confused them (14:2; 16:14). Matthew took care to repeat Jesus' own summary: "Among those born of women there has arisen no one greater than John [11:11]."

We cannot avoid the conviction that for the Evangelist the conflict with Jewish leaders (3:7-10) echoed the struggles still current in his own day. These struggles did not generate innocuous sentiments, but bitter vitriol. These enemies were branded as a "brood of vipers" (3:7; 12:34; 23:33); that is, their paternity was assigned not to Abraham, as they claimed, but to the chief of serpents, the devil. They were neither capable of authentic repentance nor willing to produce its fruits. Of all people they were most in danger of being burned up like the chaff. Nevertheless, in his vendetta against these enemies, Matthew had a more important target: his own colleagues, the prophets and teachers within the churches (7:15f.). Among them, the repentance marked by baptism could fail to produce the intended fruits. Apart from such fruits these successors to the apostles would receive no immunity to the fire of God's judgment. Matthew recognized that any vision can be killed by routine, any community can become the enemy of the very reason that brought it into existence. Every tree is vulnerable to the ax of which John spoke.

One other point is to be made about this way of telling how the story had begun. Like the first two chapters, the third chapter asserts that in the sending of John, God had fulfilled the promises as found in scripture. But also, as in the stories of Jesus' genealogy and birth, this fulfillment had been most surprising. No one had expected the great day of the Lord to dawn in this fashion. There was no cosmic fanfare, no procession of kings and potentates, no earthquake to herald the appearance of God's Messiah, no onslaught by armies of the saved. Instead of all this, God had sent an unaccredited and fantastic scarecrow, a nobody appearing nowhere, talking in scare-language about an ax and fire. To hear him, people had to drop everything and go out to the wilderness.* On the basis of John's warning alone they had to forsake all other types of security and to confess their sins, joining the riffraff of penitents who had nothing to lose and everything to gain, should this message later prove to be true. One can have great sympathy for those Pharisees. It is only natural that leaders who are most aware of the tragic dimensions of human history should be least gullible in accepting any announcement of redemption that carries with it so little evidence of change in the balance of political and economic power. Matthew, in short, discerned in this tradition about John the same mysterious contradiction as in the traditions of Jesus' lineage: a genuine fulfillment of Israel's story from the time of Abraham, which could not be discerned except by a reversal of normal expectations with regard to salvation.

To sum up, the work of John in Judea fulfilled Isaiah's prediction as did the work of Jesus in Galilee (cp. 3:1, 7 with 4:12-16). The two men prophesied in turn to Judea and Galilee, one in the center of Israel and the other in the region of the gentiles "toward the sea, across the Jordan" (4:15). Later, from Galilee, Jesus commanded his delegates to baptize all the nations (28:16-20), thus linking Matthew's readers through the apostles to Jesus and through Jesus to the baptism of John. John had made it clear that Jesus' authority to baptize would be superior to his own (3:11); Matthew also made it clear that Christian baptism must continue to embody both the promises of Isaiah and the warnings of John.†

*Cf. U. Mauser, *Christ in the Wilderness* (London: SCM Press, 1963).
†Cf. C.H.H. Scobie, *John the Baptist* (Philadelphia: Fortress Press, 1964).

The Work of Jesus (3:13—4:22)

In Matthew's conception of things, baptism and temptation belonged together. Accordingly, the Spirit that descended at the baptism led Jesus immediately into the wilderness. The sonship announced in 3:17 must be put on trial immediately (4:3, 6). Just as the test of sonship presupposed Jesus' baptism, so too the baptism was incomplete apart from this trial by Satan. Jesus had to win this struggle with the devil before light could dawn for those living in death's shadow (4:16). Moreover, to Christian scribes this decisive victory must at every point be established as a fulfillment of scripture (3:15, 17; 4:4, 7, 10).

Three types of conflict are involved in this twin event of baptism-trial. First is the implicit contrast between Jesus and the picture of the Pharisees in the previous episode. As a prophet, John had had the gift of discerning the secrets of people's hearts (1 Corinthians 14:25). In the hearts of the Pharisees he discerned subtle complacencies and hypocrisies (3:8-10); in the heart of Jesus, something quite different (3:14). The false Pharisaic claim, "We have Abraham as our father," corresponded to the claim the devil wanted Jesus to exploit: "I have God as father." If Jesus had not penetrated the devil's deception, he would have become one of the "brood of vipers." The same Pharisees later accused Jesus of using satanic powers (10:25; 12:24). This story provided the church with an effective reply, a reply especially relevant for readers whose baptism introduced them into trials like those of Jesus (6:13; 16:23; 26:41). Scribes demanded more dramatic proofs that salvation was at hand; this story corrected the illusion (12:38f; 16:1f.). Scribes required scriptural proofs that the Messiah had come; although this story appealed to the law (Deuteronomy 6:13, 16; 8:3) and the prophets (Isaiah 42:1), it also showed how the devil, like the scribes, had used the same scriptures to deceive (e.g., 4:6, citing Psalm 90:11-12). The *fruits* of repentance, so lacking in the Pharisees, had appeared immediately in Jesus, yet this was a different proof from what the scribes had expected.

The second conflict is of a different kind. This is the momentary altercation between John and Jesus, in 3:14-15, a debate between the two prophets that Matthew seems to have added to his Marcan source. The addition is usually explained as due to an increasing reverence for Jesus; Matthew did not wish to impute to the Lord any sin that might have required repentance from him. There is merit in this explanation, but another possibility may also be mentioned. The story does not so much accent the sinlessness of Jesus as the interdependence of the two men in the fulfillment of what God required. John's work had been ordained by God in line with Isaiah's prophecy. John in turn had uttered his own prophecy; Jesus now came from Galilee in fulfillment of the word of *both* Isaiah and John. In verse 14 John sees his own prophecy fulfilled, and he naturally wanted to be baptized by the Stronger One. John recognized Jesus as the source of the coming baptism, one far greater than his own. In reply to his hesitation Jesus indicated his desire to fulfill "all that God requires [v. 15, NEB; the RSV phrase "to fulfil all righteousness" has many potential meanings]"; in corroboration of Jesus' decision the Spirit descended on him; a heavenly voice announced the fulfillment of John's prophecy and that coincided with the fulfillment of Isaiah's prophecy (3:17; Isaiah 42:1; Psalm 2:7). And what a surprise! That all righteousness, all that God requires, should be realized in repentance! Such a conviction reverses all normal human ideas of religious perfection.

A third conflict dominated the story: the struggle with Satan, which would continue until the end of the Gospel and throughout the history of the church (26:41). This duel began immediately after Jesus' baptism, as an initial result of his baptism by the Spirit (3:11, 16). The place (wilderness) and the duration (forty days) echoed earlier trials God had imposed on Moses, on Elijah, and on Israel during the Exodus (Exodus 34:28; 1 Kings 19:8; Deuteronomy 6:13-16; 8:3; Numbers 14:33f). The first two tests were so phrased as to include dilemmas faced by Christians as well as by Jesus. Christians looked on themselves as children of God who had been baptized with the Spirit. They cherished teachings in which Jesus had promised them enough bread (7:7-11) and stories that had celebrated Christ's power to feed multitudes in the wilderness (14:13-21). Yet they were often faced with the danger of starvation. The prohibition against putting God on trial (4:7; Deuteronomy 6:16) had become difficult for a persecuted church to obey. Of the three temptations the struggle with the devil on the mountain seemed to Matthew the crucial one. At issue was the exercise of authority within two opposing kingdoms: God's and Satan's.* The location on a mountain is, of course, symbolic; from no mountain on earth can one literally see all kingdoms. The Matthean tradition had chosen the mountainsite as appropriate for decisive messianic teachings (chaps. 5—7; 24—25), for disclosures of transcendent authority (17:1-9; 28:16-20), for messianic prayer and struggle (14:23; 26:30), and for the exercise of redemptive powers to sustain the church (15:29; 18:12). Matthew may have understood the struggle on this first mountain as key to the messianic salvation that would later be enacted on other mountains. In any case, this opening victory of Jesus over the devil qualified him to announce the dawning of the kingdom of heaven (4:17). His baptism was now complete, for he had proved his willingness to follow the Spirit. He had demonstrated what it means to be God's son (3:17). This sonship was not to be defined by the devil's standards (or by those of synagogue scribes or fainthearted followers), but by willingness to live by God's word alone (4:4), by refusal to put God to the test (4:7), and by repudiation of self-seeking compromise (4:10).

To Matthew, this definition of sonship applied to Jesus and to his followers. The call to repent, as issued by John (3:2) and by Jesus (4:17), was a call to reject Satan's ideas of prestige and power. The story belonged squarely in the center of the conflict between church and synagogue. It sought to demonstrate that Jesus belonged to the line of such heroes as Abraham, Moses, and Job, who had overcome similar trials

*Birger Gerhardsson, *The Testing of God's Son* (Lund: C.W.K. Gleerup, 1966).

of faith. It also sought to explain how Jesus had demonstrated his power to liberate others who had come under the tyranny of the demons.

The care with which Matthew located the place of the initial preaching may reflect his special interest, because he, like many ancient writers, believed that the first event in a series prefigured all later events in the series. The dawning of light took place *in Galilee*, described by Isaiah as gentile territory, and *in Capernaum*, because this city, unlike Nazareth, was by the seaside in the territory of Zebulun and Naphtali. The promise of dawn would be fulfilled when the crowds gathered to receive the gifts of healing and of light in Jesus, an event that followed at once (4:23f.). This motif recurs in his word that the disciples were to serve as *the light of the world* (5:14, 16) and in his warning against allowing this light to be extinguished (6:22-23). The maximum penalty for "sons of the kingdom" who betrayed their calling would be expulsion into the surrounding darkness (8:12; 22:13; 25:30).

In this first instance the light dawned with Jesus' preaching (4:17) and his announcement of coming events. As one of the three activities often assigned by Matthew to Jesus (preaching, teaching, healing, 4:23; 9:35; 11:1), this preaching linked Jesus not only to his predecessors, such as Isaiah and John, but also to his Christian successors (10:7, 27; 24:14; 26:13). This preaching was in fact prophecy, the announcement of a coming, heavenly event coupled with the demand for the only appropriate response—repentance. Here Matthew was content to give an epitome of Jesus' message, probably because his own readers were acquainted with the message as a whole. Nowhere does this Gospel spell out in detail the message Jesus gave to the general public, for it was designed, rather, for church leaders to use in their work with believers, not unbelievers. These believers, with the Evangelist himself, seem to have thought of repentance as a once-for-all decisive response to the prophet's word of approaching doom (11:20-21; 12:41). Repentance was what had happened in Nineveh at the visit of Jonah. It was what had not happened in Tyre, in Sidon, or in Sodom. It was what did not happen among the scribes and Pharisees (cp. 12:38 and 3:8) or among Galilean cities, including Capernaum (11:23). Repentance was not so much a matter of inner, recurrent remorse for specific vices, as it was an act of accepting a prophet's disclosure of God's plan.

The first acceptance of Jesus' message came from four fishermen (4:18-22). They responded not simply to the message of the kingdom, but to a summons to receive special training as "fishermen." They were to form the nucleus of the twelve who, after this period of training, would become apostles (13:47-50).* Others would follow Jesus without embarking on this training and without leaving boats and family (19:27-29). Why, then, did Matthew, following the account in Mark, place the call of the four before the reference to public response? Possibly because he sensed the importance of having leaders for the "crowds" who would soon begin to follow Jesus (4:25). From this initial episode by the Galilean lake to the final episode on the Galilean mountain, this Gospel gave major attention to the special sacrifices and the special training of the twelve (of whom these four remained the prototype). As we have seen, Matthew usually distinguished these leaders, called disciples, from the much larger number of followers, whom he called the crowds. Accordingly, he introduced both groups at the outset of Jesus' preaching.

A Manual for Church Members (4:23—7:29)

In the first three verses the reader receives a panoramic view of what is to follow. Jesus will carry out a triple task: preaching, which proclaims the dawning of the kingdom (4:17); teaching, which provides instructions for followers (chaps. 5—7); and healing the maladies of humankind (chaps. 8—9). Teaching "in their synagogues" probably refers to the reading and interpretation of the scriptures and to the defense of this interpretation against the scribes. While Jesus

*Cf. W. Wuellner, *The Meaning of "Fishers of Men"* (Philadelphia: Westminster Press, 1967); E. Hilgert, *The Ship and Related Symbols in the New Testament* (Assen, The Netherlands: Van Gorcum, 1972).

did not neglect this confrontation in the synagogues, he also sought out the people everywhere, with the result that crowds flocked from a hundred-mile radius to hear him. The first geographic reference—"all Syria"—found only in this Gospel, may have been included because this was Matthew's home and the possible location of the churches to which he was writing. If so, he took this way to forge a direct link between his audience and the beginning of Jesus' work. Matthew described a public response to Jesus that was instantaneous and even explosive; great multitudes were quickly drawn from a wide area. In following him they accepted his authority and became a major audience for his teaching until the end of his mission. Whatever view is taken of Jesus' story, this view must make credible the staunch allegiance of these crowds, which Matthew set in sharp contrast to the bitter opposition of the Pharisees.

It was Jesus' concern for these followers that impelled the mountaintop lecture (5:1; 9:35). It was with them "in view" that he assumed the authoritative posture of a teacher, that of sitting down. Although he addressed his disciples, he was training them for later leadership of the crowds. This probably explains why the crowds, absent at the outset, appear at the close of the Sermon as if they had been present all along 7:28). Perhaps Matthew distinguishes the two segments of Jesus' audience by using the third person for the crowds (as in v. 3) and the second person for the disciples (as in v. 11).

The first eight beatitudes (5:3-10) form a composite description of the entire company of followers and their reward. These beatitudes constitute a single poetic structure, each sentence shaped to parallel the others, each adding a special nuance to the whole. We should probably assume that all eight describe the same group of people and that the eight rewards portray a single condition of blessedness. When read in this way each beatitude clarifies and reinforces the others. For example, those who enter into the kingdom of heaven (nos. 1 and 8, a favorite image in Matthew) are the same as the "sons of God" who receive the vision of God and enjoy God's forgiveness and comfort, the satisfaction of their hunger and thirst, and the inheritance of the earth. Similarly, poverty of spirit is to be understood as roughly synonymous with mourning, meekness, mercifulness, peace-making, and suffering persecution for righteousness' sake. All who followed Jesus were thus confronted at the beginning with the rigor of his demands and the exorbitance of his promises, understood as the immediate inheritance of ultimate salvation.

The shift to the second person in 5:11 signifies a turning to the disciples and an explicit discussion of their future, as distinct from that of followers-in-general. They are viewed as prophets, in line with earlier prophets (5:12b, also 10:41; 13:17; 23:34). Within the church they continued the task of the scribes, interpreting and teaching the law (5:19). They functioned as the light of the "house" and of the world (5:14). The words "You are the salt...you are the light" (5:13-14) on Jesus' lips are as significant to their vocation as were the words of Peter to Jesus: "You are the Christ [16:16]."* The slander and hatred these disciples would later incur would be suffered as his delegated representatives. Five times Matthew uses the phrase "for my sake" (5:11; 10:18, 39; 16:25; 19:29); in all these cases he had in mind dangers that would qualify these disciples to sit on "twelve thrones judging the twelve tribes." The chief dangers came mainly from the synagogues and their leaders (10:17-22, 35-40). Presumably, the slanders would include the charge that they wanted to abolish the law and the prophets as did their master (5:17). The warning against savorless salt may have been designed to counter the temptation on their part to placate their enemies by compromising the message (5:13). Efforts to put the lamp under a bushel may likewise have been motivated by fears of the violence that would result from speaking openly. In any case, the disciples were warned that unless their faithfulness exceeded that of the Pharisaic scribes (their counterparts as lead-

*M. Jack Suggs, *Wisdom, Christology, and Law in Matthew's Gospel* (Cambridge, MA: Harvard University Press, 1970), pp. 120-26.

ers of the synagogues) they would be excluded from the kingdom (5:20).

We discern in the Sermon, then, both a warning against yielding to persecutors and a direct denial of the charges made by those persecutors against church leaders in Matthew's own time. Even the hostility of the scribes was a fulfillment of the prophetic role (5:12), a fulfillment that should release joy in the hearts of the persecuted. In the New Testament this joy was often seen as a direct accompaniment of affliction (1 Peter 1:6, 8; 4:13; Revelation 7:13-17); it signaled the participation of martyrs in eschatological salvation (Luke 1:47; 10:21; John 8:56; Acts 2:26). Joy in suffering has ever since been a paradoxical sign of the good news of the kingdom. The kingdom that appeared to destroy the scriptures was in fact their vindication and consummation. People who appeared to practice a righteousness that was too permissive had in fact adopted standards which were far more rigorous.

Such concern with the conflict between Christian teachers and Jewish scribes probably induced Matthew to collect the four sayings about the law in 5:17-20. Originally separate, each with a different function and message, these sayings had been gathered into a single paragraph as summaries of how Jesus had treated the law. The four sayings have proved, over the centuries, to be puzzling riddles, on the meaning of which interpreters have rarely agreed. The four axioms are not consistent with one another; nor do they seem to fit the beatitudes that precede or the six antitheses that follow. Some of these latter antitheses illustrate verse 17, some illustrate verse 20; none seems to illustrate verse 18 or 19, unless the words "these commandments" refer to the teachings of Jesus that follow, rather than to the whole body of commands in the Torah.* The four axioms are broad generalizations relevant to highly polemic situations that had been created initially by Jesus' own radical behavior. They offer little specific guidance on how people should act; for this guidance, one must consult the six

*Ibid., pp. 116f.

48

antitheses that follow, as well as the episodes which tell of Jesus' own behavior vis-à-vis the law.

In his editing of 5:21-48 Matthew presented six examples of how Jesus dealt with commands of the law ("It was said to the men of old" [vv. 21, 27, 31, 33, 38, 43]). This arrangement, however, appears to be forced and artificial. It was a product both of catechetical needs within the churches and of conflicts with competing leaders of the synagogues. Each of the six probably developed separately and in response to variant needs, before being incorporated within the series. Let us examine the first four together. The first step is to separate the third (vv. 31-32) from the rest, because its form is different, it deals with a different sort of problem, and it is on a level of thinking different from the others. Because it appears elsewhere in a more natural context (19:9), it will be discussed in that context.

Three features are common to the remaining three units: (1) the positive command, or teaching, of Jesus, of which the sign is, "But I say"; (2) the negative antithesis, of which the sign is, "It was said"; (3) various expansions of one or another point.

The positive commands are almost certainly the earliest, most provocative nuclei of the traditions. "Everyone who is angry...Everyone who looks lustfully...Let what you say be simply 'yes' or 'no'." These are forthright and unqualified prohibitions of anger, lust, and deceit. The root of evil is traced to the innermost impulse, which is now judged to be itself so evil as to merit the penalty that had usually been affixed only to the external action. Presumably, Jesus' followers have accepted this absolute standard as binding on themselves; they dare not reject Jesus' authority (*I* say to *you*).

The three antitheses take the form of three direct citations from scripture, citations that already carried weighty authority: "It was said." Two citations are lifted from the ten commandments (Exodus 20:13-14; Deuteronomy 5:17-18); the third is drawn from other central collections of God's commands (Leviticus 19:12; Numbers 30:2; Deuteronomy

23:21). These citations underscore the gravity of what is at stake: For those who revere the decalogue, anger must be considered as terrible as murder, illicit desire as terrible as adultery, deceit as terrible as perjury. Another function of the citations is to relate Jesus' teachings to the Mosaic law: Those who obey Jesus' rule (e.g., on anger) would certainly fulfill the legal standards as well (e.g., on murder) and would even achieve a righteousness superior to that of the scribes. Therefore, Christian scribes (v. 19) must not relax this standard but must obey it and must teach their "students" to obey it.

Expansions of the three core teachings appeared at several points. In two cases the expansions took the form of providing several examples of the actions forbidden (vv. 22, 34-36). In two cases the expansions took the form of telling what people should do if they discovered that they had broken the new rules (vv. 29-31). In another case instructions were given for altering the situation that had induced anger (vv. 23-24); another insertion clarified the kind of behavior one should adopt when being sued (vv. 25-26), a situation only obliquely related to the core teaching on anger. These expansions illustrate the type of casuistry that becomes necessary as soon as teachers who have been charged to enforce difficult standards must give advice on how to apply these rules to the varied situations that emerge within the daily routines of a religious community.

In the last two antitheses (5:38-48) Matthew arranged a cluster of seven commands on how to deal with other people— with borrowers, beggars, robbers, persecutors, litigants, and other types of "enemies." Five of these commands Matthew grouped under the category of how to respond to evil actions (vv. 39-42); two of them under the category of how to deal with enemies (vv. 44).*

This classification was accompanied by the choice of two citations with which a teacher should contrast the new stan-

---

*For the form of these commands, cf. Robert C. Tannehill, *The Sword of.His Mouth* (Philadelphia: Fortress Press, 1975).

dards. These citations were introduced by the phrase, "It was said...," but it is difficult to locate the precise reference of these citations (e.g., a command to hate an enemy). In the case of retaliation a command can be found (Exodus 21:24; Leviticus 24:20; Deuteronomy 19:21), but it seems to be on a level different from the others. It was not one of the primary prohibitions of the decalogue. In these two cases Jesus seems to have rejected the law; it presented commands that his followers should not obey, contrary to the statements in 5:17-18. Such inconsistency may have come from the editorial effort to force these teachings on the love of enemies into conformity with the formal pattern of the earlier antitheses.

What I have called expansions in the case of the earlier antitheses are not so obviously present here, probably due to the fact that this collection was well developed before Matthew used it. We have seven examples of merciful responses to the actions of others, not all of whom need be evil people or persecutors. Each of these seven, however, undercuts a person's self-interest by forcing the person to give priority to a neighbor's or an enemy's needs. By extending the same principle one could multiply the examples seventyfold and cover the whole gamut of human relations. The same motive was advanced for all seven (vv. 45, 48), the desire to become children of God. It is by behavior like God's that men and women become God's sons and daughters. Moreover, a common foil was provided for all seven, not in this case the law, but rather the behavior of tax collectors and gentiles, who presumably limited their love to those who reciprocated this love. All this was directly germane to Matthew's situation, in which the enemies of the disciples (v. 44) were Pharisaic scribes who attacked them as enemies of the law. By loving and praying for these persecutors, Christians could prove they were not as lawless as Jewish tax collectors or pagan gentiles.

The study of the next passage (6:1-18) is aided by an analysis of its formal structures. (A more detailed analysis appears in Supplement 2.) The skeleton is provided by three carefully organized stanzas (vv. 2-4, 5-6, 16-18). The three stanzas deal in turn with three practices characteristic of synagogue piety: philanthropy, prayers, fasts. In each case the wrong mode is first prohibited, after which the right mode is enjoined: "When you give alms, do not...when you give alms, do...." Each line of each stanza parallels similar lines in the other two stanzas; the repetition is most apparent in the last line of each: "Your Father who sees in secret...." There is, to be sure, variety in the descriptions of conduct, whether ostentatious or secret; but this variety is occasioned by differences in the kind of piety. Trumpets can be used to attract attention to almsgiving, but it is "dust and ashes" rubbed into the face that advertises fasting. By contrast, maximum secrecy is secured, in the case of almsgiving, when one hand is unaware of the other's generosity or, in the case of prayer, when a person is alone in his or her room. Yet these differences in depiction do not disturb the symmetry of the three stanzas; nor do they deflect attention from the identical point made in all three. Together the three stanzas drive home a pattern of behavior that can be applied to all forms of religious observance.

To this skeletal structure four other items have been drawn by the operation of various forces (vv. 1, 7-8, 9-13, 14-15). Verse 1 was added to provide an introductory summary covering all three stanzas. As such it is deficient in that it supplants the vivid imagery of the stanzas with a prosaic and banal warning; and by focusing on the negative element it misses the positive promise.

The next accretion (vv. 7-8) was attracted to this setting by the theme of praying; it adds a second type of praying that is to be avoided—the verbose jabbering of gentiles. Here we discern the efforts of Christian scribes to help their communities develop a third way, distinct from both Jewish and pagan types of piety. The repudiation of the pagan type served also as an added rebuttal against the slanders from enemies in the synagogues.

The next addition (vv. 9-13) brings into this context the prayer Jesus gave his disciples. The collection of these various teachings on prayer was no doubt useful to both scribes and their students, even though to place this prayer here interrupted the pattern of the three parallel stanzas. Moreover, this public prayer collides with the call for secrecy in praying (v. 6). The simplicity and brevity of this corporate prayer was probably seen as a contrast to the gibberish of the gentiles (v. 7), but it does not fully accord with the principle advanced in verse 8. The prayer has been shaped at least partially by liturgical practices within the churches. Desires have shrunk into simple and succinct petitions; they follow one another in a natural sequence that moves from concern for God and God's kingdom to the basic needs of daily life, set within the context of the struggle with the evil one, i.e., the devil.

The last addition (vv. 14-15) was attracted to this setting by the petition in the Lord's Prayer for forgiveness. It is a balanced aphorism (if you forgive...if you do not forgive) that stated a principle universally affirmed within the early church and universally attributed to Jesus.

Looking back over this collection of commands we notice several recurring accents. For example, a pervasive fear of hypocrisy in religion intrudes whenever one gives social prestige priority over one's standing with God. It is assumed that the slightest desire for public notice destroys the authenticity of any religious action and automatically substitutes reward from fellow humans for reward from God. The basis for this teaching is the conviction that God demands from every person an unqualified sincerity and integrity.

Along with this demand the teachings disclose a quite distinctive understanding of God's will and ways. No fewer than ten times does the name *Father* appear, and always with the plural possessive pronoun, *your*. Together the teachings provide a many-sided conception of what constitutes both fatherhood and sonship. The fact that "your Father knows" is absolutely essential. God's presence in all places and times is never in doubt, for God "sees in secret." Likewise, God's power and love are assumed to be always in operation. God's forgiveness or refusal to forgive (vv. 14-15) is assumed to mark the difference between salvation and damnation.

The definition of sonship is consistent with this picture of fatherhood (continuing the thought of 5:45-48). Persons become worthy of sonship by an honesty that permeates the most secret thoughts and desires, and by a communal living in total confidence (v. 8) and total dependence (vv. 9-13). A level of religious life is described that seems utterly opposed to the routine practices of formal institutions. How long could organized charities survive if all donors remained unaware of their contributions? Or how long could the practice of fasting continue if there were no way of separating those who were mourning from those rejoicing (v. 17)? If every type of social pressure were removed from any religious duty, how long would observances persist? We may have here the most potent attack on the religious establishment to be found anywhere in the Bible, an attack for which Jesus claimed the full authority of "the Father," who required perfect integrity on the part of all "his children." It was the early church that accepted and preserved these antiestablishment rules, according to which only two options are open to a church and its members: either hypocrisy or the heart purged of pretense.

In the next symmetrical stanzas (6:19-24) the blunt choice between two options is made inescapable: *either* earthly *or* heavenly treasures, *either* the healthy *or* the blind eye, *either* mammon *or* God. These choices reinforce those offered in the previous section: reward either from fellow humans or from God.

6:19 Do not lay up for yourselves treasures on earth, where moth and rust consume and where thieves break in and steal,

20 but lay up for yourselves treasure in heaven, where neither moth nor rust consumes and where thieves do not break in and steal.

21 For where your treasure is, there will your heart be also.

22-1 The eye is the lamp of the body.

2 So, if your eye is sound,

3 your whole body will be full of light;

23-4 but if your eye is not sound,

5 your whole body will be full of darkness.

6 If then the light in you is darkness,
7 how great is the darkness!
24-1 No one can serve two masters;
2 for either he will hate the one and love the other,
3 or he will be devoted to the one and despise the other.
4 You cannot serve God and mammon.

Verse 20 is the opposite of verse 19, a result achieved by the alternation of heaven and earth and by the addition of negative adverbs. This is an excellent example of antithetical parallelism, as is also the contrast between lines 2 and 3 of verse 24 and between the sound and the unsound eye. Synonymous parallelism is illustrated by lines 1 and 4 of verse 24, which say the same thing in two ways, although line 4 makes the reference to love for money more explicit and thus serves as the conclusion. Verse 21 is a way of repeating verses 19-20, making clear that the location of the heart is determined by its treasure. The parallelism in the "eye" saying is a bit different. Line 1 establishes the basis for the contrast between the two visions. Line 7 carries the thought of the contrast a step further to its conclusion in an exclamation.

These teachings have caused difficulty within the church from the beginning. They express an evaluation of wealth that flatly contradicts all usual estimates, and they do so with the uncompromising authority of Jesus. Note that Jesus' primary concern was with the location of the heart or the light of the body or the undiluted service of God. Of course, in making such rigorous demands Jesus possibly had in mind the special requirements of disciples whom he was training as "fishers of men" (cp. 10:5-15, 37-38). Even so, he also required these teachers to present the same demands to all followers without diminishing their rigor. As leaders, teachers might face distinctive occupational hazards, but sooner or later those who accepted their gospel would be required to carry the same cross. The Evangelist relayed this teaching to his readers without diminishing its force.

He followed it with equally forceful prohibitions of anxiety (6:25-34). When we ask what would be the circumstances in which these commands against anxiety were most urgent, the answer points to the dilemmas faced by the twelve after they had been sent to the cities of Israel as sheep in the midst of wolves. As penniless mendicants, they would be dependent on unknown hosts for each day's food (10:9-11). The command not to fear persecutors (10:28f.) parallels this prohibition of anxiety and even uses the same comparison of missionaries with sparrows. Close parallels can also be found in the autobiographical notes of an apostle (2 Corinthians 6:4-10; Philippians 4:11-13). Anxiety over food and clothing was also rife among the laity within virtually every congregation; every class of catechumens, as well as more mature Christians, had to be ready to face economic destitution and social ostracism. The injunction of 1 Peter 5:7 was always relevant: "Cast all your anxieties on him, for he cares about you." Especially would times of stress be likely to strike those who took seriously the commands of 5:37-48, including the requirements of unlimited almsgiving (5:42; 6:4). Worry about food might well increase when a believer had given away his or her money (e.g., Ananias in Acts 5). Overcoming such anxiety would be a tough test of how one had in fact made the choice between two masters. The reality of such worries prompted teachers to bring into one paragraph a number of separate sayings on anxiety.

Verse 34a is an independent proverb, a pithy axiom like many that circulate orally in numerous cultures. In form a tiny chiasmus (a, b, b, a) it embodies a dose of common sense. It was attracted to this cycle by the theme of anxiety, although in motivation there is nothing distinctively Christian about it (but it would fit well in the context of 10:9-13). The grim reminder in verse 34b that today has a full quota of trouble seems even more alien to the trust in God's care which characterizes the other sayings. These twin axioms accent the contrast between today and tomorrow, whereas the earlier commands focus on the conflict between self-concern and confidence in God's care.

The central and most substantial teaching is the prohibition in verse 25, supported by the twin parables of the birds (v. 26) and the field flowers (28b-30). Listeners were identified in verse 30 as "men of little faith," a characteristic way of describing disciples who were wanting in courage and confidence (cp. 8:26; 14:31; 16:8; 17:20). That Matthew had them in mind is implied by the phrase "your Father," by the loaded reference to the gentiles, and by the call to seek the kingdom. Their troubles would spring from the dangers of the mission on which Jesus intended to send them (chap. 10); if these dangers induced panic, it would prove their lack of faith both in the mission and in the God who had sent them. To be sure, these twin parables could possibly be seen as expressions of an unsophisticated and uncritical reliance on popular, superstitious views of divine providence.* Rather, the verses contain a grim realism that echoes the struggles of a martyr community. Birds were a symbol of frailty and helplessness (cp. 10:29) rather than of security and strength. So, too, the abrupt destruction of grass was noted in such a way as to do away with any romantic notions of their own immunity to a violent death (v. 30; cp. Isaiah 40:6-8). Birds and grass are indeed dubious proofs of God's care, in view of their cheapness and transiency. Their very expendability makes these parables all the more germane to a poor, persecuted minority in a world that scoffed at their weakness and folly. In this string of sayings, then, we can overhear Christian leaders trying to quiet anxieties produced by discipleship, using to this end various appeals that had been inherited from Jesus.†

For the assortment of teachings in 7:1-14 we should visualize as an audience both the smaller company of disciples and the larger company of followers, corresponding to the teachers and laity in Matthew's churches. Several of the teach-

*So Rudolf Bultmann, *History of the Synoptic Tradition* (New York: Harper & Row, 1963), p. 104.
†Cf. Soren Kierkegaard, *Christian Discourses* (London: Oxford University Press, 1940), pp. 11-93, 313-56; *Gospel of Suffering* (Minneapolis: Augsburg, 1948), pp. 166-236.

ings had special relevance for the scribal teachers (e.g., the prohibition of judging [vv. 1-5]). The scribes in the synagogue had been trained to serve as judges in disputes under criminal, civil, and religious law. The same tasks were inherited by scribal teachers within the church; they had been chosen to sit on thrones "judging the twelve tribes [19:28]." A more detailed picture of disciplinary procedures appears in the Manual of Discipline (chap. 18). The opening verse, "Judge not, that you be not judged," is a radical prohibition of condemnation, like the commands in 5:43-45 and the parable in 18:23-35. Those who condemn others make themselves hypocrites. The log in one's own eye is formed automatically by the action of condemnation, because it contradicts the unlimited mercy of God. To condemn a brother or sister is to be condemned by God's mercy.

The Evangelist next turns to a cluster of sayings that would be especially appropriate to wandering charismatics as they sought hospitality from town to town (10:11). The core of this cluster is found in the triple command-promise of verse 7: "Ask, and it will be given you; seek and you will find; knock, and it will be opened to you." Each command is embodied in a single sharp word that addresses listeners as a group (the *you* is plural). Each command leads to a promise appropriate to the action: When a person knocks the response is an opened door. Each command reinforces the others, like the sides of an equilateral triangle. The three sides are so briefly and symmetrically shaped that the saying can be easily memorized, and had been memorized by Christians before it was placed in this Gospel.

The core saying was followed by a triple axiom (v. 8) and a twin parable that illustrates the command to ask (vv. 9-11). This analogy turns the whole unit into a teaching on prayer, whereas the triple command and axiom had a broader reference. The special circumstances faced by church leaders may be reflected in the request for the bread and fish (vv. 9-10) that it was the special obligation of "deacons" to provide for communal meals (15:34f.). Moreover, the kind of total dependence on God for daily sustenance the teaching enjoins was especially relevant for itinerant prophets and messengers (10:9-25).

The command in 7:12, later called the Golden Rule, is also especially relevant as a defense against scribal accusations ("the disciples of Jesus defy the law and the prophets"). As such it is a fitting conclusion to the debate begun in 5:17-20. It shows Matthew's conviction that the law and the prophets were fulfilled not so much by theological argument as by merciful behavior in which the grace of God (7:11) had become the basis for all human action. The verses which follow (13-14) indicate that, contrary to the accusation that Christians made things easier, the new way was much more difficult than the righteousness of the scribes and Pharisees (5:20).

A large part of this manual was devoted to distinguishing the righteousness of the poor in spirit (5:3) from that of the Pharisaic scribes (5:17-20) and also from that of the gentiles. Although Jesus' commands were more rigorous than the others' (7:13-14), they were also more liberating and more merciful. This paradox has always been difficult to maintain, especially among ambitious church leaders. Both members and genuine prophets were forced to be on their guard against wolves dressed in sheep's clothing. Verse 7:1f. might seem to exclude heresy hunts, but the presence of daily dangers confronting the churches required expertness in discerning which of the visiting prophets were trustworthy. Often they came with high credentials, asserting their commitment to Jesus with the reverential term Lord (reduplicated in v. 21 for emphasis). Often they exercised impressive prophetic gifts (visions of heavenly reality), along with the power to exorcize demons (in fulfillment of 10:8). At times they accomplished works that were as spectacular as those of Jesus (11:20-23; 13:54). Could such beneficial fruit be harvested from "thistles"? (v. 16). This passage warns the churches to be wary of these credentials. Such gifted prophets could be workers of lawlessness *(anomia)* who would be repudiated by him at the final accounting. How could Christians test their own leaders? The requirement of *good fruits* in verses 16-19 was not fulfilled by the impressive beneficial works listed in verse 22. Prophets and teachers could authenticate their positions only by obedience to "these words of mine," that is, to all the commands, implicit and explicit, in 5:3—7:12 (N.B., the repetition of *these words* in vv. 24, 26, 28). Genuine sheep obey; wolves, driven by their inner greed, disobey. Although they are Christian, they have in fact adopted the selfishness and the hypocrisy of the Pharisees. (Compare the sins of disciples, attacked here, with those of the Pharisees in 23:23-28.) It is significant, then, that the conclusion of the Sermon on the Mount should express so forcefully this attack on the potential hypocrisies of those whose task it would be to make these rules binding on all followers of Jesus. To refuse to obey these commands would mean a rejection of Jesus' authority, and that would bring about certain exclusion by Jesus from his presence (v. 23). The Sermon ends with a parable intended to clinch every word Jesus had uttered.

Chapter IV

~~~

THE PHYSICIAN AND THE CROWDS

Cases of Therapy (8:1—9:34)

The crowds that had formed the secondary audience for the manual of membership (7:28-29) now become the primary audience in several stories of healing. The first (8:2-4) discloses Jesus' power to cleanse a person of leprosy, a condition that, in New Testament times, included many types of skin diseases viewed as evidence of religious defilement. According to this story, Jesus took care to observe the legal provisions for the termination of ritual defilement. Matthew regarded this emphasis as an instance of Jesus fulfilling the law (Leviticus 14:2) and the prophets (8:17; Isaiah 53:4). The point was not simply that Jesus had had the power to heal, but that he had accepted and bore "our diseases." Coming down from the mountain of revelation and instruction, he had entered the valley of the shadow of death. His own willingness to carry the burden of pain, ostracism, and defilement had been symbolized by his gesture of touching the leper. This act had made Jesus as unclean as the leper had been.

A second instance of healing (8:5-13) also involved ceremonial defilement, inasmuch as the centurion was a gentile. To help him would be an act of political disloyalty, inasmuch as he was a commander of the hated occupation army. The centurion's sensitivity to this point was one measure of his faith (v. 10) as well as of his meekness (v. 8). His attitudes exemplified several beatitudes and commands in the Sermon (e.g., 7:7-12). The story of the healing thus served to symbolize several things: Jesus' compassion for the paralyzed servant, his ability to recognize great faith on the part of the gentile soldier, his sharp warning to "the sons of the kingdom," his declaration that the coming kingdom already fulfills God's earlier promises to seat gentiles at table with the patriarchs.

A leper, a gentile, a woman—these were three types of people on whom Jesus had compassion. All three were viewed by Jesus' contemporaries as untouchables, as outsiders, or as insignificant. What was significant was not simply Jesus' ability to heal sickness, but his readiness to defy social and religious taboos. This readiness was as miraculous and even more obnoxious to fellow Jews than the fact of the healings. The declaration in verses 11-12 was nothing milder than a declaration of war on those who relied on the patriarchs as their ancestors. Matthew makes it quite clear that it was easier for Jesus to expel demons from their homes in people than to rid his scribal enemies from their taboos.*

The editor's comment on these stories shows how he viewed Jesus' work not as an abolition of the scriptures, but as a fulfillment: "He...bore our diseases [v. 17]." By the phrase *our* diseases, Matthew called attention to the bond between the crowds in Jesus' day and the followers in Matthew's day. The later churches were composed of folk whose heavy burdens had also been lifted by Jesus. Finally, the transition to the next paragraph, "when Jesus saw great crowds" (8:18; cp. 5:1), indicates that it was his concern for the crowd that impelled Jesus to call and train scribes to serve as physicians. Later these disciples would be authorized to do the same mighty works in Jesus' name (10:5f.).

In 8:18, Matthew directed the attention from the crowds to the disciples. The decision to embark on a mission trip to gentile country became a fitting occasion for teaching the kind of sacrifices that discipleship entailed. They must abandon their homes for the sake of continuous travel, accepting the same homelessness as the Son of man (v. 20). They must

---

*An excellent treatment of Jesus' miracles may be found in E. and M. Keller, *Miracles in Dispute* (Philadelphia: Fortress Press, 1969).

substitute the demands of the new "family" for the obligations to parents under the old regime (v. 22). As requirements of their special calling, these conditions reflected the radical newness of the situation created by the nearness of the kingdom.

The Gospels considered that a boat was an ideal place for training fishermen (4:21-22).* This particular journey by boat was described in highly symbolic language. The winds and water symbolized the ominous power of evil, whereas the boat suggested the apparently weak resources of God's people in their combat with evil. The fear and faithlessness of the disciples matched the violence of the storm, whereas the poise of their master corresponded to the quieting of the lake.† Their panic proved their unreadiness to lose their lives for his sake, and thus their cry became the petition of those desperate for salvation. Jesus' reply manifested his power to save and their need for faith in him. (Similar accounts in 14:13-33 indicate that the training in faith had moved partway toward Jesus' goal.)

Jesus' first mission to pagan territory was also described in highly symbolic language (8:28-34). A group of demons immediately resisted his invasion into their jurisdiction, realizing that he had come to terminate their power even ahead of schedule. Where could they go if they could no longer inhabit the two gentiles? Jesus first used his power to free the two men from their uncleanness (they had been forced to live in the cemeteries) and from their insanity (they had frightened everyone away), and he then agreed to let the demons enter the herd of swine (the acme of uncleanness for Jews). The drowning of the swine in the sea (the source of evil) represented the return of the demons to the primeval home of all those powers that from the beginning have resisted the creative work of God. Gentile owners of the swine were shocked at this example of Jesus' power. They said in effect,

*E. Hilgert, *The Ship and Related Symbols in the New Testament* (Assen, The Netherlands: Van Gorcum, 1962), pp. 84-90.
†Gunther Bornkamm, et al., *Tradition and Interpretation in Matthew* (Philadelphia: Westminster Press, 1963), pp. 52-57.

"If this is what salvation costs, let's have no more of it." Did Matthew intend to invite reflection on the kinship between the fears of the disciples and the reactions of this pagan city, or the kinship between the evil powers that caused the sea storm and the sea that swallowed the demons and the swine? Like many stories in the Gospels, this one is rich in allusions, few of which can be reduced to precise statement. The implications of Jesus' first mission to a gentile region, however, would not escape disciples who, after his death, continued to preach in similar places and who had to wrestle with demonic forces.

The liberation of the crazed gentiles in an alien city was followed by the cure of a paralyzed Jew in "his own city" (9:2-8). (Capernaum was regarded as Jesus' home during the Galilean ministry [4:13; 8:5]. Unlike Nazareth, Capernaum was located on the lakeshore. Mark 2:1 makes the identification of Capernaum and "his own city" clear.) Readers should not overlook several accents that accrue from the location of this episode:

1. This was the first occasion in Matthew where the scribes mounted an attack leveling the same charge as that on which the high priest later called for the verdict of death (26:65). The charge was provoked by what appeared to be exorbitant claims for the Son of man, in this case his assertion of the right to forgive sins.

2. The response of the crowds is the opposite (v. 8), for they recognized that the power to forgive had been given by God. The use of this power therefore was good reason for them to glorify God. The same crowds sensed that the capacity to heal paralysis could be traced to the same authority which had been expressed on the mountain (cp. v. 8 and 7:29).

3. Two things are made clear in verse 6. The basic authority had been that of forgiving sins, for it was this forgiveness which had enabled the paralytic to walk. Moreover, this authority had been exercized on earth, implying that the source of authority had been located in heaven, and that the Son of man was serving as mediator between heaven and earth. His access to prophetic knowledge of the thoughts of

people (v. 4), along with his ability to recognize and forgive sin, had been manifestations on the earthly level of heavenly reality.

4. The faith of the men who had brought the paralytic to Jesus had been one clue to the victory over paralysis. Here, as elsewhere, the accent falls more on the intercession of others than on the sick person (cp. 8:6f.). This faith, so unlike that of the scribes, had been fully endorsed by the crowds.*

In the next section the center of interest shifted again from the crowds to the disciples (9:9-17). The shift took place when Jesus called a customs collector to join the company of disciples. The call of Matthew introduced both the table scene (9:10-17) and the ordination of the twelve disciples in 10:2f., where Matthew is also mentioned. The dinner with Matthew provoked two debates. One debate was introduced by a Pharisee's protest to the disciples about their Master's table companions; the other grew out of a question by John's disciples about his disciples' behavior. One dealt with festivity, the other with fasting.

One has difficulty visualizing how all three groups could have been present at a single table (v. 10); but Matthew was not concerned with such a difficulty. The theological issues were more important than preserving journalistic realism. The protest by the Pharisee provided an opportunity for Jesus to explain his eagerness to eat with sinners, i.e., to demonstrate the truth that God prefers mercy over sacrifice (Hosea 6:6). The work of mercy included the forgiveness of sinners and the healing of the sick (the two are identical here as in 9:5). From this work the Pharisees had excluded themselves; to this work Jesus and his disciples were committed. Matthew the sinner was fully qualified to serve as a disciple.

The next debate developed the theme of joy as opposed to that of mourning over sins, as expressed in fasting. The meals Jesus ate with his disciples and with the crowds of hated tax collectors and despised sinners were like wedding cele-

*For these and the other miracle stories in Matthew see H.J. Held in ibid., pp. 165-299.

brations. A bridegroom and his guests do not mourn; they rejoice. Because this metaphor of a wedding feast had long been used to describe the joys of the messianic age, it here conveys the conviction that when Jesus ate with tax collectors and sinners he was fulfilling the messianic role, these being his guests at the wedding. The new age has dawned. The new wine, now being harvested, should therefore be put into new wineskins (v. 17).

With the next section (9:18-34) Matthew returns to the cycle of healing stories; in this context the cures now become further examples of extensions of mercy by this physician (v. 12), further reasons why fasting should give way to festivity. These stories are linked to 11:2 and to 11:4: "Go and tell John what you hear and see," for they now see "the dead are raised up"—the central sign in 9:18-26—and "the blind receive their sight" (9:27-31, 11:5). These stories also illustrated the two sides of the prophetic blessing in 11:6. The crowds were blessed because they took "no offense" (9:26, 31, 33). But not so the Pharisees (9:34). In chapter 9 we find only this brief indication of scribal opposition; in chapter 11 it becomes a major factor. In this context of popular gratitude and scribal hostility the healings served to illustrate the saving power of faith. This interpretation was accented by the story of the blind men who hailed Jesus as the son of David and therefore as one who could relay divine mercy. For Matthew, it was the exercise of this mercy that qualified Jesus as the son of David. Faith was also central to the story, and although faith was not mentioned in the case of the ruler, his confession bespoke full confidence in Jesus' power. These stories had long circulated among Christians who identified themselves with those whom Jesus had made whole; these stories were a rough equivalent to such later hymns as Charles Wesley's "O for a Thousand Tongues to Sing":

> Hear him, ye deaf; his praise, ye dumb,
> Your loosened tongues employ.
> Ye blind, behold your Savior come,
> And leap, ye lame, for joy.

The texts should not be read as journalistic reports supplied by observant bystanders, but as symbolic stories in which believers told what had happened when, in their desperate need, they had received divine mercy. They supposed that only two lords could wield power over demons: either the prince of demons or the messiah sent to liberate people from them. They viewed their own situation as a continuation of the same tasks in which the twelve disciples had been engaged (10:1). This, at least, was Matthew's attitude, for he placed the manual of instructions for physicians at the center of this cycle of healing stories, introducing the manual by a summary of the cures produced by the great Physician (9:35-38).

A Manual for Physicians (9:35—11:1)

The order in which Matthew arranged this summary probably reflects his own distinctive accents. The whole mission of Jesus (his travels, teaching, preaching, healing) is declared to be motivated by his compassion "for the languishing and leaderless people."* Further, the same compassion dictated the call and the commission of the twelve to serve as shepherds of the same flock.† The choice of the flock image is significant. This image had long been used to describe Israel, God's covenant people (Numbers 27:17; 1 Kings 22:17; Isaiah 53:6; Ezekiel 34:5). Their one-time shepherds, the Pharisaic scribes, had played truant, leaving them scattered and exposed to "every disease." The appearance of a new shepherd was the signal for a new epoch in the story of the flock; the extension of his work required that he authorize the twelve to be his delegates. Their work as teachers had been described in the Sermon on the Mount; now their work as preachers and healers was detailed in this ordination sermon (10:7-8). This was the first occasion when Matthew used the number twelve for the disciples, a number indicating that all twelve tribes were included. Earlier they had been de-

*Bornkamm, et al., *Tradition and Interpretation in Matthew*, op. cit., p. 18.
†Cf. Paul Minear, *Images of the Church in the New Testament* (Philadelphia: Westminster Press, 1960), pp. 84-89.

scribed as fishermen; here they were described as shepherds, harvesters, and healers. The healings were understood to be one form of the harvest, one activity by which shepherds gathered together again "lost sheep of the house of Israel [v. 6]." The church in Matthew's day welcomed this story as describing its own origins, and thought of itself as sheep cared for by successors to these shepherds.

In his list of the twelve (10:1-4) the Evangelist helped his church to celebrate the memory of these original shepherds. Only once (v. 2) did he call them apostles; more commonly he called them "the twelve" (10:5; 26:14, 47) or "the twelve disciples" (10:1; 11:1; 20:17; 26:20). Most often he spoke of them simply as the disciples (about sixty times). In most instances where he used this simpler designation, Matthew had in mind the group of twelve to whom Jesus gave a special role as shepherds and physicians.

All synoptic lists began with the two pairs of brother fishermen, Peter being named first;* all closed the list with the betrayer. Matthew listed the same names as Mark in virtually the same order. He showed a shade more interest in Peter by explicitly applying to him the adjective *first,* and in Matthew by identifying him as the tax collector, whose call he had already described (9:9). His prime concern was not with the names (six of the names do not recur in this Gospel), but with their commission; in his own day it continued to be the commission that was the important thing. The number twelve had its own importance, for it expressed faith in the salvation of all Israel (twelve tribes) in line with the promises given to the twelve patriarchs, the sons of Jacob (Genesis 35:10-15).

This manual for physicians (beginning 10:5) answered many questions that later disciples would raise. In what should their work consist (vv. 7-8)? How should they support themselves (vv. 9-10)? Where would they find lodging? How should they respond to rebuff (v. 14)? The answers were grounded not only in Jesus' words, but in his own practice (vv. 24-25).

*R.E. Brown, K.P. Donfried, J. Reumann, *Peter in the New Testament* (Minneapolis: Augsburg, 1974).

Guidance was needed in Matthew's day because of the desire on the part of itinerant prophets to develop a less demanding type of life. Within the later churches, reliance on itinerant prophets was diminishing in favor of greater reliance on resident leaders (Didache, XI). The greater rigor embodied in this manual is a token of the urgency and finality of their prophetic journeys. Response to these wandering charismatics would be as decisive for the towns they visited as for Sodom and Gomorrah, because "the kingdom of heaven is at hand."

The explicit limitation to "the house of Israel" has caused difficulty for interpreters precisely because it seems to restrict Jesus' horizons to parochial dimensions. However, the commission to all nations, in 28:16-20, proves that this apparent limitation did not exclude a universal mission. Then why the restriction here? Because Jesus had limited his own mission in the same way (15:24; although we should not forget 8:10; 12:18, 21)? Because of Jesus' immediate concern for the shepherdless flock of 9:36? Because even Paul, the missionary to the gentiles, had recognized that Israel had come first in God's plan (Romans 1:16; 2:9; 3:1; 9:1-6)? Because there were in Matthew's day Christian leaders who wished to abandon the mission to Israel because of its danger and apparent futility, even though such a termination would have been in direct repudiation of Jesus' concern for this flock? All answers remain conjectural. Much more certain is the fact that during the earliest period the twelve fishermen did in fact concentrate their efforts on preaching and healing in Israel. Because Matthew believed that the disciples would sit on twelve thrones judging the tribes of Israel (19:28), a rejection of their message was considered tantamount to exclusion from the Israel to whom Jesus had come as shepherd. On their part, gentile converts were viewed as authentic initiates into the life and legacy of Israel. Here, as in the earlier sections, Matthew insisted on the fulfillment of God's promises to Israel and on the wholly unexpected forms taken by this fulfillment.

The hazards stressed in the next cluster of sayings (10:16-33) were those that characterized Jewish hostility to Christian prophets in Matthew's day. To be sure, Jesus had faced some of these same hazards. He had been called Beelzebub. He had been delivered up to at least one council and had been dragged before the governor at least once. Despite betrayals, he had endured to the end, fearing only God (v. 28). He had thus validated his testimony before Jewish judges and gentile rulers (v. 18). No trial people would face in later generations would exceed his agony (v. 24). Yet the details of Jesus' struggle also fitted the later situation when Matthew was trying to coach Christian scribes to accept martyrdom at the hands of synagogue leaders (cp. 23:34). Jesus had not only foreseen this prospect, but had willed it as an essential feature of their work. Authentic witness to synagogues and to gentiles required venturing like sheep into a den of wolves. How else could the gospel message be proclaimed from the housetops? The issue was not whether to avoid hostility or to accept it, but how to utilize the opposition as a means of accomplishing their task. Would they yield to hysteria (v. 19) or endure persecution, confident of vindication by the Son of man (v. 23)? Would they covet greater immunity than his (v. 24), allowing the fear of people to displace the fear of God (v. 28)? Or would they use each crisis as the occasion for preaching and healing (vv. 7-8)? The dominant accent in this collection of commands falls on the principle of identification with Christ (vv. 32-33). If people acknowledged him (i.e., by accomplishing the same task in the face of the same hostility), he would acknowledge them before the ultimate Judge of Israel.

In 10:34-39 Matthew was still concerned with the martyrdom of Jesus' emissaries. He makes it clear that such martyrdom, far from being an unforeseen and unfortunate exigency, had been consciously intended by Jesus in his role as savior. Jesus had come with a sword to set everyone at war with one's family, to test the strength of the competing loves. The question of whether a person shared the martyrdom of Jesus had become the measure of whether this person was really worthy of Jesus. In this context the aphorism concerning losing and finding life received a sharp and clear definition. Perhaps this chapter should be called a manual for martyrs.*

In verse 40 Matthew's attention shifts from the twelve apostles to their hosts, and from the apostles' enemies to their friends. The earlier predominance of references to hostile reception (vv. 14-39) indicates a situation in which the breach between synagogue and church was almost irreparable. The preservation of verse 40, continuing the theme of verse 13, indicates that church leaders were still finding a favorable response here and there among their Jewish neighbors. Here the principle of identification is extended to include those who offer hospitality to the wandering prophets. The hospitable act established solidarity among four distinct persons: "the one who sent me," "me," "you-the-twelve," "your hosts." The two intermediate persons (you, me) are essential, but the ultimate goal is to show the bond between the ones who receive Christian prophets and the God who sent Jesus.

The same logic may underlie verses 41-42. If so, the *Revised Standard Version* translation obscures this logic. "He who receives a prophet *because he is* a prophet" focuses attention on two agents alone—the host and host's guest. "He who receives a prophet *in the name* of a prophet" is a more literal translation that allows the notion of three agents, parallel to those in verse 40. In this case a host entertains as a guest a prophet who has been sent by another prophet. By his act of hospitality the host confesses his faith that both the wandering preacher and the one who sent him (Jesus) are authorized spokesmen of God. Such a host is promised "a prophet's reward" from God, for he has in effect extended his hospitality to God (v. 40). Similarly, the host who entertains a righteous man in the name of another righteous man will receive the reward of both the commissioner and the missionary. In this case, "righteous man" may have carried in Matthew's vocabulary the force of the modern word martyr. It was applied

*D.R.A. Hare, *Jewish Persecution of Christians* (Cambridge, MA: Harvard University Press, 1967), pp. 96-113.

by Matthew to Jesus in connection with his Passion (27:4, 19, 24); it was also applied by inference to the twelve (13:17) and to their successors (23:29, 35). Often appearing in conjunction with prophets, the term "the righteous" could refer to those who vindicated their loyalty to God by vicarious suffering. The context of chapter 10 would seem to refer most naturally to those who had suffered the hazards so vividly described, hazards that carried the rewards stipulated by Jesus, whether to the twelve or to their successors.

The same logic is carried one step farther in 10:42, provided that the phrase "little ones" refers to ordinary lay members, and the term disciple, in whose name the lay member is received, refers to one of the traveling missionaries. Should this interpretation be correct, these verses (40-42) yield vivid pictures of the early church in which the offer of hospitality—whether to Christian laity or to Christian prophets (outside agitators)—carried acute risks and merited special praise from Jesus. Of this praise the most effective expression in the Gospel is the parable of the Last Judgment (25:31-46), which illustrates the granting of the promises advanced in 10:40-42.

Because the work of these spokesmen for Jesus had become so important for Matthew and his readers, I should perhaps summarize the picture provided by this chapter. How is their work described? They serve as shepherds (9:36), harvesters (9:38), healers, preachers, exorcists, beggars, sheep, serpents, doves, sparrows, criminals, refugees, prophets, slaves. What a galaxy of epithets! What a range of tasks! Some of these epithets reflect their relationship to Jesus, some to the crowds, some to their enemies.

What was the relation of the twelve to Jesus? They were called by him because of his compassion for the *crowds*, to extend his work of teaching, preaching, healing (9:35; 10:7-8). For these tasks he gave them full authority, the same authority he exercised (10:1). They proclaimed the same news, being sent to the same house of Israel. Like him and by him they were given awesome power to mediate God's peace or judgment to every house, village, and town. They viewed every home as capable of salvation or damnation. As members of Jesus' household they were met by the same libels as he—the same hostility, hatred, and martyrdom. The teacher set the pattern for every disciple, the lord for every slave (vv. 24-25). In his name and with his power they would act, whether in raising the dead or in being hated. The sword with which they provoked warfare within each household would be his sword (v. 34), just as was the peace they would pronounce on hospitable hosts. To be worthy of him they must carry their crosses, losing their lives for his sake (v. 39). Their representation of him was so complete that for a person to receive one of the twelve was the same as receiving Christ, and this meant welcoming God. Moreover, every action or word by which they would acknowledge Christ before people would be acknowledged by him before his Father. The chain of command and authority, of responsibility and of accountability, was tightly woven. Christ intended them to continue his mission as in some sense his *alter ego*.

How did this manual of instruction relate the twelve to the harvest field? Jesus was not so concerned for the twelve as for the field, the sheep who were harassed and helpless. The twelve must share his concern for the sick, the demon-driven, the leprous, the dead. They must not omit any Israelite village from their itineraries. They must not charge for their services, any more than Christ had charged for his (v. 8). They must travel as poor, helpless, friendless wanderers, without any claim to hospitality other than the good news of the kingdom. When they met opposition, they should respond without anxiety, relying not on any visible credentials, but solely on the support of the Spirit. Their journeys would often require their use of courtroom or gallows as pulpit. They must not seek out easier places to preach or expect the kingdom to dawn elsewhere than in these centers of rebellion. Only by such work could they bring home to Israel the ultimate decisiveness of the call to the kingdom of God. By this response Israel would be divided and either blessed or cursed. Such was the work of these twelve shepherds, as they faced a kaleidoscope of changing situations (at least twenty distinct settings can be distinguished).

How could their credentials as apostles be tested? Essentially, every situation became such a test. But their credentials could not be any more obvious than those of their master. Their credentials combined three elements: the authenticity of their commissioning by Christ; their faithfulness to his charge, his example, his mission; the results of their work as measured by hostility and by hospitality. How did Jesus safeguard his choice of the twelve? Not by advance specifications and occupational surveys. Not by avoiding the selection of outcasts or traitors. Not by providing security and fringe benefits. But by sending them on the road to face obstacles similar to those he faced. Their credibility as *his* disciples would be of the same order as his credibility as Messiah.

Chapter V

THE MYSTERIOUS PRESENCE
OF THE KINGDOM

Separation of the Violent from the Gentle
(11:2—12:50)

How did Matthew understand the connections between chapters 11 and 12 and the preceding manual (chap. 10)? Chapter 10 had predicted a double response to the work of the twelve; now that same double response greets the mission of Jesus: rejection by synagogue leaders (11:12-24) but welcome by the "babes" (11:25-29). The preaching of the kingdom (11:1) produced signs that bewildered the unrepentant cities (11:20f.) but attracted the gentle and lowly. These signs had the power to produce hope among the gentiles; yet this power could be attributed to the devil as readily as to God (12:24). The question, "Can this be the son of David?" evoked such divergent answers as to pose another question: "Why are the secrets of the kingdom revealed to some and hidden from others?" (13:11). One group took offense at Jesus' work (11:6; the word offense is a strong word, connoting such instinctive and total repudiation as is reflected in identifying Jesus with the devil); the other group, who had ears to hear (11:15), received such rest for their souls (11:29) as to become members of Jesus' own family (12:50). The stories in these two chapters show how this division actually took place.

In three episodes (11:2-19) Matthew related the work of John to the work of Jesus. (In an earlier source these may have been connected to a fourth episode now found in 9:14-17.) The first paragraph (11:2-6) presented an answer to John's question in terms of Jesus' preaching and healing. It admitted the likelihood of offense and proclaimed the beat-

75

itude of those who accepted the good news that was both concealed and disclosed by the signs. This story echoed a period in the life of the early church when people knew disciples of John who had not accepted Jesus as "the one who was to come" (Acts 19:1-7).

The second paragraph (11:7-15) represented an irenic effort on the part of the church to preserve Jesus' high evaluation of John. It indicated that the same people who accepted Jesus as a prophet had earlier accorded the same authority to John. Both men had been sent from God to announce the dawning of the kingdom; both had come in fulfillment of prophecy. The prophetic work of John had marked a major transition in God's plans for Israel, inasmuch as he had come in the role of Elijah (Malachi 3:1; 4:5). Although Matthew recognized an important difference between John and "the least in the kingdom," his chief accent here falls on a high appraisal of John's role. John had prepared the way; therefore, Christians should never repudiate his work.

The third paragraph continued this defense of John by implying that his deeds had been produced by the same "wisdom" as the deeds of Jesus. John and Jesus had, to be sure, followed quite different styles of operation. John, like children weeping at funerals, had practiced prolonged fasting. His enemies had accused him of using demons to supply his food during the fast. Like children dancing at weddings, Jesus had called for festivity. His enemies had confused this joy with drunkenness. The two prophets had aroused hostility from the same group, the same wisdom had been repudiated by the same people. Each of the three paragraphs ends with a pregnant but ambiguous axiom (6, 15, 19c), which underscored this double response to the prophets' message.

Both John and Jesus had presented "signs" that demanded repentance, yet both had encountered rejection. This rejection had been similar to the earlier reactions of Tyre, Sidon, and Sodom; accordingly, there would be a comparable condemnation in the final judgment (11:20-24). Implicit in this tradition was the belief that Jesus' message had been in line with that of earlier prophets; this is why the coming day of judgment would see all cities of all epochs receiving their condemnation simultaneously. Here we touch on a basic characteristic of biblical thinking about time; one final day would somehow cover many different times. By its rejection of any true prophet at any one time, a city became liable to the same penalty that would be inflicted on all rebels at all times.

Chorazin is mentioned only in this Q dialogue (Luke 10:13-15), an apparently casual reference to a city that must have been a center of Jesus' activity. Many other towns probably did not receive even this much mention in the records. Bethsaida left only a slightly deeper trace (Mark 6:45; 8:22). As Jesus' hometown, Capernaum was better known (Matthew 4:13; 8:5; 17:24), but the rarity in the records of such geographical names indicates how little interest the early church exhibited in matters of this sort. Much greater interest was shown in Tyre, Sidon, and Sodom, because in legend these places had become symbolic of terrible destructions at the hands of God (Isaiah 14:13f; Amos 9:2; Obadiah 4; Habakkuk 2:9; Psalm 139:8). To Matthew, any city—however small or remote—could become a new Sodom by its behavior (Revelation 11:8).

At 11:25 the editor again registered a sudden shift from enemies of the gospel to its friends, from the hardhearted to the openhearted. The shift took the form of a brief prayer of this son to his Father, a prayer of thanksgiving in which Jesus approved this division of all persons into "wise men" or "babes." He traced both acceptance and rejection of the kingdom to God's gracious decision either to hide the truth or to reveal it. Here Matthew adopted an attitude that was common among Christian interpreters (e.g., John 12:37-43; Romans 9:14-17; 11:5-12; 1 Corinthians 1:26-29; 1 Peter 2:4-8) who needed a way of explaining the sharp contrast in public response to their own work—on the one hand, the avalanche speed with which thousands accepted the Gospel and, on the other, the volcanic force of hostility to it. The truth is, of course, that few movements in history have had such rapid growth in the face of such bitter opposition. Matthew was writing at a time when observers were trying to comprehend both developments.

At 11:27 the form of discourse changed. Here the Son proclaimed with full authority his unique relationship to the Father: "All things have been delivered to me by my Father." This fact had been hidden or revealed in the preceding events. In view of the hiddenness from "the wise" (i.e., Jesus' enemies), the recognition by "the babes" of his sonship could only have been a result of divine influence (cp. 16:16f.). Such recognition in turn had opened the way to an utterly unique knowledge of the Father. In disclosing to human beings his sonship, Jesus had disclosed to these same "babes" a wholly new understanding of God's will.

A proclamation like this seems to fit best a situation in which Jesus was visualized as speaking to a worshiping congregation.* These words articulated the mysterious redemptive role of a savior who had established a new covenant between his people, himself, and his God. The proclamation of verse 27 turned naturally into the call to discipleship of verse 28f.: "Come to me, all who labor." This invitation was one way by which Matthew's audience described the impulse that had led them to accept the "yoke" of this teacher. Accordingly, this paragraph, by using imagery drawn from many Jewish traditions of wisdom, was able to describe how Jesus had been able to communicate the knowledge of his father to "the gentle and lowly in heart."† That this invitation should later have become widely used as a call to worship is not surprising; it had already been shaped by the liturgical experience of the yokefellows in the Matthean churches.

In chapter 12 attention shifted back to the "wise" from whom God had hidden the truth. The first occasion was con-

---

*Cf. Soren Kierkegaard, *Training in Christianity* (London: Oxford University Press, 1941), pp. 9-42.
†M. Jack Suggs, *Wisdom, Christology, and Law in Matthew's Gospel* (Cambridge, MA: Harvard University Press, 1970), pp. 71, 97.

flict over sabbath laws with the Pharisees, who, as defenders of the commandments (Deuteronomy 5:12-15), had finally determined to destroy him. The issue was whether Jesus and his disciples were justified in working on the sabbath. This issue was probably still current in Matthew's day, so Jesus' reply to his enemies would be seen as useful in the later situation. Jesus combined four separate arguments, each with a distinctive set of implications:

1. The precedent of David and of those who were with him (1 Samuel 21:1-6) is claimed for Jesus and for those who were with him. This precedent, however, could be cogently claimed only if Jesus, as messianic son of David, exercised authority comparable to David's, and only if his companions were essential partners in his work.

2. A different precedent is advanced by the reference to the priests (vv. 5-6). Although they work on the sabbath and thus break the law, they incur no guilt because of the special provisions needed for the care of the holy place (Numbers 28:9-10). If immunity be granted to the temple, it should also be granted to Jesus and his companions, because something greater than the temple "is here."

3. God's desire for mercy takes priority over God's regard for temple offerings. Because the disciples were hungry their sabbath labor is justified as an act of mercy; their attackers are guilty of refusing such mercy.

4. As the Son of man, Jesus holds a position as lord of the sabbath. Whenever people act in obedience to his command, the breaking of the sabbath laws is warranted. This seems to imply that the Matthean church did not deny the validity of the sabbath laws, but it is entitled to set them aside for good reasons.

In these incidents we encounter again the issue Matthew has dealt with from the beginning: How can the mission of Jesus be considered as the fulfillment of the law and the prophets when it so obviously seems to contradict any such fulfillment? "It cannot be so considered" said the wise of 11:25 and the Pharisees of 12:14. "It must be" said the babes, along with their defender, the Evangelist. But obviously, they could defend this answer only by recognizing that in this instance God gives priority not to the legal prohibition, but to the "value" of a person and to the demand for mercy (v. 12). In taking this position, of course, these babes recognized that Jesus was now exercising an authority to disclose by what actions the law is truly fulfilled. In this episode the example of a sheep that had fallen into a pit may have been intended to call to mind the image of Israel as lost sheep and the parable of a shepherd searching for his hundredth sheep (18: 12-14).

At first the next paragraph (12:15-21) appears to strike a different note. Yet when we are made aware of Matthew's continuing concern with showing how the work of Jesus polarized the nation, this contrast is not surprising. Rejection of the gospel by Jewish leaders had from the beginning (3:5-10) seemed to fan the enthusiasm of the crowds, and this enthusiasm in turn whetted the fears of the leaders. Rejection by the Pharisees was thus linked to the divine plan for the salvation of the gentiles (vv. 18, 21). What appeared to be disobedience to the law opened the way to the fulfillment of the law and the prophets (in 12:7 it is the word of Hosea; in 12:18f., the word of Isaiah). The withdrawal of Jesus from the synagogue to "the crowds" probably corresponded to the shift from Jewish to gentile mission on the part of the early church, a shift made clear in the account of Paul's mission, in Acts (e.g., Acts 13:44-52). Isaiah's prophecy (42:1-4) illustrated not only God's response to the rejection of his servant, but three other points as well:

1. In those who followed Jesus could be seen the fulfillment of God's promise to the gentiles.

2. The phrase "he healed them all" (12:15) represented the gift of divine justice and hope to people who otherwise had neither.

3. His command "not to make him known" (12:16) fulfills the description of this servant of God as a nonaccredited, nonviolent messenger, who would rely more on silences than on noisy speeches; "Nor will any one hear his voice." His command to silence indicated that they should respect the

reasons why God had hidden from the wise Jesus' authority as lord of the sabbath (12:8) and his sonship to David (12:23). In other words, to those expecting the Messiah, no one would seem to be less qualified than he.

It was no wonder, then, that Jesus' healings could be explained in either messianic or demonic terms; the crowds of followers gave the first appraisal, the Pharisees the second 12:22-45). According to Matthew, this ambiguity was fully in line with Isaiah's prophecy, fully in accord with Jesus' choice and with his instructions to his followers. However, this by no means excused those who chose the second appraisal. In this long passage Matthew collected a dozen or more sayings of Jesus that condemned the blindness of the Pharisees. Some of these sayings apply to the point at issue (what authority does he have over demons?); others are unrelated attacks on Pharisaic hypocrisy. All echo the bitter warfare between synagogue and church during the first generations. Many of the sayings are generalized denunciations. The Pharisees, by not "gathering" the flock with the Shepherd, scatter it. They are guilty of blaspheming the Holy Spirit. Their words are the evil effluent from evil hearts. By demanding signs they prove themselves guilty of adultery, the conventional prophetic metaphor for having a husband other than God. They are "clean houses" into which a demon has brought seven other spirits more depraved than itself. As a brood of vipers, their fate in the final judgment will be worse than that of the people of Nineveh or the queen of Sheba (Jonah 1:2; 3:4; 1 Kings 10:1-10). As "an evil generation," it is they and not he who are children of the devil.

Mixed into these denunciations are other sayings that defended Jesus and, by implication, Christian exorcists against the charges leveled by their enemies. Success in expelling a demon displayed a use of power against Beelzebub and therefore presupposed a strength greater than his. The Spirit of God is Satan's enemy, and the exercise of the Spirit's power is tantamount to the coming of the kingdom. Exorcisms show that the kingdom of God is close at hand; but as signs they are as ambiguous as the sign of Jonah (12:39). They are cogent only in calling people to repentance. Refusal to repent is the root blindness of the Pharisees. In this long debate with the Pharisees (cp. chap. 23) Matthew has combined many teachings that seemed to him to explain what Paul had called "the hardening of Israel's heart" (Romans 9:19—11:12).

Growing hostility made even more amazing the degree of loyalty to Jesus on the part of the crowds. At two earlier points the account had stressed the contrast between unrepentant cities and repentant crowds (11:20-30), and between Jewish legalists and gentile libertarians (12:9-21). Now the story turns to the contrast between the brood of vipers on the one hand, and the family of God and God's children on the other (12:46-50). The two groups may be distinguished by their paternity. The family of Jesus become children of the same Father by doing the Father's will. Their adversaries become offspring of vipers (12:34; Jews commonly spoke of the devil as a serpent). In identifying *the twelve* as Jesus' family, Matthew deviates from Mark, who spoke of the *crowds* as the family (Mark 3:31-35); yet Matthew does not limit this family to the twelve, but uses the inclusive indefinite pronoun whoever. The twelve have specific roles as teachers (as chap. 13 makes clear), but in their teaching they should make clear to the crowds (a word wrongly translated as *the people* in v. 46) the requirements of all the followers of this Messiah.*

As told in all three Synoptics, this story appears to imply a degree of rejection of his immediate family by Jesus. Did his mother and brothers oppose his ministry? Did he repudiate his ties to them? The Synoptic story, however, was not so much interested in such questions as in announcing the radical creation by Jesus of a new family. It was also concerned with making clear the duties of the disciples to the crowds, because this relation would continue in the life of the church. Once the Evangelist had described the polarizing process by which the message of the kingdom had separated the violent

---

*Paul Minear, *Images of the Church in the New Testament* (Philadelphia: Westminster Press, 1960), pp. 165-72.

from the gentle, he could move on (in chap. 13) to set forth in parables the mysteries of the kingdom that Jesus had revealed to the twelve for the benefit of the crowds.

One further word by way of summary. I believe chapters 11 and 12 were designed to prepare readers for chapter 13 in this way: Those two chapters showed how the message about the kingdom of God divided the audiences of Jesus into followers who were willing to die for him and enemies who were eager to plot his death. How is it that the same message produced such opposite results? Why did the same actions on Jesus' part prompt such an understanding and such a total misunderstanding? As Christians pondered these questions they came to realize that the kingdom of God itself is inherently a great mystery. The response to this mystery is what separates the "wise men" from "babes." Chapter 13 concentrates on the intrinsic character of this kingdom.

A Manual of Kingdom Secrets (13:1-52)

The third major sermon of Matthew was given from a boat to crowds of followers standing on the beach. The sermon was composed of parables that Jesus addressed to the crowds but explained to the inner circle. The parables—seven in all—were concerned with the kingdom of heaven (3, 24, 31, 33, 44, 45, 47). Greatest interest—as judged by length, location, and separate explanation—is focused on the first two and the last. Jesus used parables to fulfill the prophecy of Psalm 78:2 (13:35). Parables are ways of declaring hidden things, riddles that do not yield to the normal empirical analysis of events (cp. 11:25). The kingdom and its signs have been hidden from unrepentant cities (11:20-24) and from scribal leaders who ascribed to the devil what had really come from God (12:24f.). Why does the prophetic message create such violent antagonism? Why has so great an impasse developed between enemies and friends? As Matthew understood the situation, it was especially necessary for the twelve scribes of the kingdom (13:52) to be instructed in these secrets so they might be more faithful than their predecessors had been (12:38f.). They must be able to discriminate between the agents of Beelzebub and the agents of God.

In explaining the first parable (v. 18f.) Jesus distinguishes four types of yield from the same seed, describing these types in detail. This sowing may be identified with the proclamation of the kingdom by John, by Jesus, by the twelve in fulfillment of the commission in chapter 10, and even by the prophets of Matthew's day. The first type of response, in which the devil prevents the message from being understood, may refer to the unrepentant cities of 10:14f. and 11:20f., to the treasonable scribes of 12:24f., or by logical extension, to the synagogue leaders of the later period. The second and third types of response (rocky ground, thorns) describe major reasons for defections among believers who have earlier responded with joy to the message of the kingdom. Because of their allegiance to the "word," the conditions described in chapter 10 become increasingly difficult to endure, and they lose heart and fall away. The first type could not understand the message. Because the second and third types could not accept persecution, they were enslaved by "the cares of the world." The fourth type accepted the message and its costs and so could produce fruit, although in varying proportions.

One may detect in Matthew's version a special interst in the two extreme groups: those who hear but do not understand (v. 19) as contrasted with those who hear and do understand (v. 23). This twofold opposition—the conflict between scribes of the Pharisees and scribes of the kingdom— is discussed in the intervening paragraph (vv. 10-17). Such residual knowledge of the secrets of the kingdom as the Pharisaic scribes once had has been taken away. Their lack of understanding has become total (v. 13) and has thus confirmed the truth of the gospel by fulfilling the prophecies of Isaiah (6:9-10). In this explanation of the seed sown along the path, Matthew continued the anti-Pharisaic polemic of chapter 12. By contrast, the seed falling on good soil continued the line of thought in such passages as chapter 10, 11:25-30, and 12:15-21. The parable assumes that Jesus, as the sower par excellence, had fully known and fully accepted the conditions of sowing; by implication it attributed to divine providence those very difficulties that Christians were facing a half century later. The parable stressed the importance of understanding the kingdom secrets, a gift Christians expected of their teachers. Although a negative reaction was foreseen by God, failure to understand was viewed as a result of the devil's malice (v. 19), manifested in blindness, deafness, dullness.

Three more parables (13:24-43) are put before the crowds as examples of the riddles of Psalm 78:2. All compare the kingdom to the act of a person who releases certain energies into society. Only one of these three parables elicits an explanation sufficiently interesting to lead Matthew to include it. This explanation turns the parable into an allegory that transparently illustrates conditions within the church. The problem is that of teaching leaders how they should react to the shocking discovery that both children of the devil and children of the kingdom exist within the church (the question of paternity so central in chap. 12). Church leaders were asking, "Who should pull up the weeds?" To this query the parable gives a clear answer. The Son of man who has sown the good seed will take care of the children of the devil at his own harvesttime. Accordingly, leaders must "let both [weeds and wheat] grow together until the harvest [v. 30]." Churches bewildered by internal conflict must learn that the mixture of good and evil within the church had been anticipated by their Lord; that mixture does not jeopardize the ultimate triumph of the righteous (v. 43).

Parables five and six (13:44-46) teach that the kingdom is so valuable that everyone must give it absolute priority (6:33), so valuable that everyone should be willing to pay whatever it might cost. Parable seven (13:47-50) warns against the danger that a person might be excluded at the last moment. This danger, in fact, is most real for those who have already been caught in the net (members of the church). Perhaps Matthew placed this warning last in the series because of his fear that the new scribes might prove as fickle as the old. So he had Jesus ask them the vital question at the end:

Have *you* understood? To understand the secrets of the kingdom was no easy matter. They needed to know why the kingdom should elicit such hostility from people, why so many of its seekers ceased seeking, why children of God should be mixed up with the devil. As we have seen, the entire Gospel of Matthew was designed to train scribes for the kingdom of heaven. This purpose is central to chapter 13.

Chapter VI

THE CARE OF THE CROWDS

Training Disciples to Feed Them (13:53—16:12)

It is difficult to sift out any principle of organization in the chapters that intervene between the manual of kingdom secrets (chap. 13) and the manual of discipline (chap. 18). We find an album of snapshots, depicting various episodes that seem to follow one another haphazardly. One reason for this is that Matthew here followed closely the order of Mark 6:1— 9:32. Matthew included twenty-one episodes, of which all but two (16:17-19; 17:24-27) had appeared in Mark in the same order. Moreover, with few exceptions (Mark 8:22-26) all the Mark material was repeated in Matthew. One assumes, therefore, that the interests of these two Synoptists coincided in dealing with these episodes.

Even though these stories appear disconnected we may notice a common denominator of concern among them. The geographical locale is much the same—Galilee, Jesus' own country (13:57), with occasional trips across the lake or to the boundaries of Tyre and Sidon, or to Caesarea Philippi. This period represents the final "gathering in Galilee" before departure for the Holy City (17:22). The shadows of what would happen in Jerusalem have begun to fall. A dramatic heightening of tension is evident in the stories of recognition and transfiguration, in which the road to the cross is clearly set forth. Moreover, there is a significant shift in the audiences. The disciples (probably the inner circle of twelve) are present in eighteen of the pericopes, whereas the crowds are present in only six and the Pharisees in only five. This suggests a strong interest in the training of these scribes "for the kingdom of heaven" (13:52).

We may recall the earlier outline of their missionary duties (chap. 10). Matthew has just finished his account of their initiation into the secrets of the kingdom (13:11). Jesus has promised to increase their knowledge (v. 12a) and has declared them blessed because of what they see and hear (vv. 16-17). In line with this initiation he announces their further training for the kingdom of heaven (v. 52). Now the development of their power to bind and to loose becomes central. Once this power was granted (16:18f.) they must be trained in its use (18:15-20), although clearly they are not yet ready to exercise Jesus' authority. Indeed, this very deficiency is perhaps the strongest motif in these narratives. This fact encourages us to ask at each step what bearing an episode has on the training of the twelve.

The first episode (13:53-58) gives an opportunity for them to learn from Jesus' experience in Galilee, where their own work would be done. They should not be disheartened when shunned by their relatives and neighbors, or when lack of faith makes the work of healing impossible. Such a reception would in fact be an omen of the validity of their message to the heartland of opposition, the hometown synagogue (cp. 10:14; 11:20).

The story of John's death was an even more instructive omen (14:1-12). Innocent of crime and despite Herod's wishes, John had lost his life as a result of his prophetic denunciation of sin. The crowd's reverence for him had not given him immunity from cruel death. Readers of Matthew would recall not only Jesus' death, but also that of various apostles and even some of their own leaders (23:23). This story would underscore the fact that every prophet of this kingdom must be able to endure unmerited persecution (13:21). Only suffering can qualify teachers to convey the truths of this kingdom.

The report of John's death became the occasion for Jesus to withdraw by boat to a wilderness. The story of what happened there is highly symbolic of Jesus' relation to the crowds and to his disciples (14:13-21). Neither group was deterred by the fate of John; each group became more determined to follow Jesus into the wilderness, which was traditionally the place of danger, of testing, of fasting, of struggle with the devil, and of strength received from God. For Christians familiar with the scriptures, it recalled the forty years en route to the promised land, when Moses provided manna from heaven for hungry refugees. It also recalled the period when the Messiah had learned to rely not on miraculous deliverance from harm, but on God's ability to sustain life (4:18-22). The enthusiasm of the crowds and Jesus' compassion for them echoed a similar setting in 9:35, where Jesus also had acted as shepherd of his flock (cp. Psalm 23). The story now, however, focused attention on the dilemmas of the disciples. The tiny supply of food belonged to *them;* it was they whom Jesus expected and even commanded to feed the thousands. At first unable to do their duty by the crowds, they were helped by Jesus to accomplish the task; the vast crowd ate and was satisfied. There is little doubt that readers would associate this story with their own eucharistic meals: the food, the representatives of Jesus (as deacons), the sitting down in orderly fashion, the prayer of invocation and blessing, the liturgical acts of breaking the bread and giving it to the people, the gathering of fragments, the "satisfaction" of those who had hungered for the bread of life, and then the benediction given by the Lord. Matthew intended his readers to see the analogy between this Galilean meal and their own suppers. Those who celebrated the sacramental suppers should understand their dependence on Jesus and their duty to feed his sheep (24:45-51).

These sacramental meals in Matthew's churches must also have reminded worshipers of other parallels between the situations in Jesus' day and their own. They knew what it was to follow Jesus into the "wilderness" of ostracism and hostility. The "Herods" of their day remained enemies with power to kill. Hunger remained so constant an experience that reliance on God for daily bread was a necessary feature of existence. Without frequent help from their shepherds the flocks would quickly lose the courage requisite for life in this wilderness.

In the boat scene that follows (14:22-36) the reader's attention focuses first on Jesus as he controls the winds and waves. Actually, the spotlight should fall as much on the disciples—or better still, on the dependence of the disciples on their commander. As in the previous story, attention is called first to the defect in the disciples' faith and then to the correction of this defect. "He made them get into the boat" suggests that Jesus had planned this step in their training. The boat (symbolizing the church [8:23f.; 9:1; 13:2; 14:13; 15:39]) moved into the deep waters (symbolizing the stronghold of evil), where it was buffeted by strong winds and high waves (suggesting the frightening upsurge of opposition [as in 10:10f.]). At the point of greatest darkness (another symbol of maximum danger) they were so panicked by their fear that they failed to discern his identity. Jesus identified himself and called for courage. As fickle and fumbling spokesman for the twelve, Peter put to the test Jesus' power over the storm. Jesus passed the test but Peter failed miserably. Fear overcame his faith. Even then Jesus saved Peter and the others from the storm. The whole story was a mirror in which Christian leaders could see themselves in the place of Peter, could receive new courage, and could face their crises with confidence. Only after such crises had been mastered could the confession of Jesus as God's son carry its full weight. When read in this way the story becomes a fascinating parable of the relation between faith and salvation and of the mysterious absences and presences of Jesus with his companions. When storm struck was he absent? or present? And how did awareness of his presence allay their fears? Thousands of teachers have experienced the truth of this parable.

The summary of cures beyond the lake (14:34-36) is typical of other summaries in this Gospel. Typical also is the shift of Jesus' concern from training future leaders to healing present diseases. Readers may notice the sharp contrast between the response in this place and in Jesus' own town (13:58), and the subtle contrast between the faith of these men and the disciples' doubt. Whereas the disciples had failed to recognize him in the midst of the storm, these folk recognized him so clearly as to bring to him all their sick. Worth noting is the reference to the fringe of Jesus' clothes, a mark of the pious Jew and especially of the teacher (23:5). The wearing of this fringe had been commanded by Moses, as a reminder of the need to obey all God's orders (Numbers 15:38-41) in gratitude for deliverance from Egypt.

Now the Evangelist returned to the issue that had been present from the beginning of the Gospel. Did Jesus teach the observance or the defiance of the law (15:1-20)? We may note the presence of the same triangle of forces. There are the scribes, carrying authority from Jerusalem to enforce obedience of the law. There are the disciples, whose behavior has given offense. And there are the crowds (15:10), to whom Jesus wants to convey the basic principle concerning defilement. Does it defile a person to eat forbidden foods or with unwashed hands? The issue was particularly acute while the church was drawing to itself Jewish members in cities where synagogues were strong. Christian teachers encountered difficulties at three levels: their debates with synagogue leaders, their instructions to the laity concerning the observance of such rules, and their disagreements—often sharp—with fellow teachers. This anecdote takes up Jesus' own response to the three needs, with accent on the third.

In the debate with the Pharisaic scribes, Jesus immediately took the offensive, accusing them of disobeying God's commandment, not to mention gross deception and fraud. They had permitted children to avoid their filial obligations by dedicating certain moneys or properties to the temple. Jesus did not deny that his disciples transgressed long-standing traditions concerning ceremonial defilement, but he charged his enemies with flouting the more important fifth commandment. Leaders with hearts so far from God could not be trusted as teachers.

The scene then shifted briefly to the crowd of followers (the laity in Matthew's churches). Here Jesus announced the radical principle of defilement, in verse 11, that he wanted them to hear and to understand: Only what comes out of the heart can defile a person (cp. 13:13-15, 19, 23, 51). As Mark had noticed, this principle had the effect of declaring all foods clean (Mark 7:19), and thus of making all dietary rules obsolete. The Jewish-Christian audience to whom Matthew was writing would have seen immediately that, in Jesus' view, no person could be made unclean by eating unclean foods. With one stroke this principle undercut all rules concerning ceremonial defilement.

The shift to an audience of disciples, in verse 12, shows Matthew's preoccupation with them and their tasks. Peter was fully aware that this teaching (v. 11) had been taken by the Pharisees as a declaration of war. What should the twelve do? Jesus' answer was blunt: "Let them alone; they are blind guides [v. 14]." It was more important for Christian teachers to understand the principle underlying the new teaching. (Peter's lack of understanding in vv. 15-16 parallels his lack of faith in 14:30, and the disciples' inabilities in 14:17 and 15:33.) They must teach the crowds that the only source of defilement is the heart. The actions and attitudes forbidden in verse 19 all come from the heart, like the sins banned in 5:21-22 (murder) and 5:27-30 (adultery). In this teaching the Pharisaic scribes played the role of negative example: Christian scribes were *not* to be blind like them. This authoritative ruling on defilement alienated the church from the synagogue and increased the difficulties that church leaders encountered in a place like Syria. This is not surprising, because the insight concerning the origin of all defilement is so radical as to destroy not only earlier Jewish legalisms, but later Christian legalisms as well.

One may ask why Matthew placed the fascinating story of the Canaanite woman at this specific point (15:21-28). Leaving the hostile scribes who had come from Jerusalem, Jesus goes to the borders of Tyre and Sidon. Is there a symbolic significance in his itinerary? Does this recall his prophecy that in the day of judgment it would be more tolerable for Sodom than for these Galilean cities? (11:24). Is this an instance of how faith can transform racial and religious walls into doors? Does the story draw a sharp contrast between the hypocrisy of the Pharisees and the honesty of this woman? Does it make clear why and when Jesus turned from Jews to gentiles (the Canaanites were traditional enemies of Israel)? Because Jesus' reply, in verse 26, seems to bespeak anything but compassion, the incident has long created a problem for interpreters. Why should he be so callous? We may not be far wrong in saying that the incident poses three tests: (1) the disciples were tested and failed to show the slightest degree of mercy; (2) the woman was tested and succeeded in displaying a faith so much greater than that of the scribes as to disclose that she was in fact one of the lost sheep of Israel (cp. 8:10f.); (3) Jesus was tested and succeeded in learning that his vocation to Israel did indeed include the mediating of divine mercy to Canaanite women. In any case, the healing of the daughter signifies simultaneously the mother's humble faith, the healer's mercy, the redefinition of the house of Israel, and the Lord's rebuke of his disciples.

Although the Evangelist had accepted the mission to the gentiles, he remained an Israelite at heart. He noticed that the gentile woman called Jesus *Son of David,* a tacit recognition of Israel as the elect people; so, too, he stressed as the primary result of Jesus' healing ministry the fact that gentiles "glorified the God *of Israel.*" Moreover, he treated these cures as confirmation of Israel's prophets (15:29-31). The importance of this new wave of cures and this new feeding (vv. 32-39) is signified by the location on a mountain (the Greek word is the same as in 5:1; 14:23; 17:1 and 28:16). Is this the same lookout from which the Messiah had seen all the earth's kingdoms (4:8)? At any rate, this is a place where authority is assumed by the act of sitting down, and a place where Jesus' concern for the crowds impels him to summon his disciples (as in 5:1). Perhaps in the earlier feeding the crowd had been Jewish, whereas on this occasion the crowds included gentiles (the contrast between twelve and seven in the number of baskets may suggest this). If so, the role of the twelve remains the same. The story offered them a case study of how to show compassion by using their resources to feed his followers.

Readers of this section of the Gospel are usually bewildered by the sequence of the stories. What sense can be made of the discussion of signs? (16:1-12). The miraculous multiplication of loaves and fish would seem to be a stupendous sign, yet the Pharisees did not see it as such. Did their blindness consist of the fact that the feeding of the four thousand had not been miraculous? Did this event come about in such a way as to blind them? What was the sign of Jonah? a prophetic announcement of doom, or the death and resurrection of Jesus (cp. 12:40)? Did their evil consist of demanding a full array of credentials before they would accept Jesus as a legitimate messenger from God, or was their adultery a matter of misinterpreting his message? One thing is sure: Whereas they insisted on testing Jesus, he turned the tables and attacked their qualifications to interpret events. They relied on signs but lacked the ability to see or interpret them.

Even deeper quandaries are posed by Jesus' discussion with the disciples (16:5-12), which seems to be an intended sequel to the wilderness meal and to the Pharisaic debate. The blindness of the Pharisees now serves as a warning to the disciples not to eat the same bread. A basic equation is this: leaven = teaching. The disciples (leaders in the later church) were in danger of accepting the Pharisees' teaching instead of Jesus'. His *teaching* in fact had been *bread,* which Jesus had used to feed the multitude. The twelve had failed to perceive this truth, and their failure meant that they had accepted the Pharisaic leaven, i.e., the Pharisaic teaching requiring the Messiah to present the kind of signs they would recognize as such. So interpreted, the story warns the twelve *not* to interpret the healing and feeding miracles as providing the kind of signs the Pharisees had expected of a Messiah. What kind of teaching could have satisfied the hunger of the crowds? This story thus forced the disciples (and the readers of the Gospel) to search for deeper meanings in the two feedings. To think of the bread as literally bread rather than as teaching would be a mistake. To make this error would be a proof of little faith rather than of strong faith (cp. 14:31). Here, as elsewhere, Jesus was dealing with a mystery that God had hidden from the wise but had revealed to the tired and hungry (11:25-30), a mystery that the disciples did not yet grasp. Jesus' effort to remedy this deficiency seems to become the point of the following episodes.

Revealing the Keys to Messianic Power (16:13—17:27)

The long fifth section of the Gospel describes how Jesus trained the twelve for their future work as teachers, shepherds, rulers of the church. This training focused on certain deficiencies in their understanding of events and therefore in their abilities to minister to the crowds. They were not yet able on their own to feed the flock, to surmount stormy seas, to discern the source of defilement, to locate the lost sheep, or to avoid the leaven (teaching) of the Pharisees. This same deficiency is reflected in the well-intentioned but mistaken protest of Peter (16:22). Here Peter served as spokesman for the twelve (and for Satan) when he rejected the idea that the Son of God must suffer. By implication he also rejected the necessity for martyrdom on the part of disciples. Such a truth was too unpalatable for Peter and for those for whom he was spokesman. Yet Jesus placed his whole authority as Messiah behind the truth that he must himself be killed and that every follower must lose his life. By juxtaposing this teaching to the preceding paragraph (omitting Mark 8:22-26) Matthew probably wished to intimate that Peter, in this instance, had consumed the Pharisaic leaven. In any case, the twelve, by their blindness to the need for suffering, had become the instruments of Satan. Such blindness could not be healed in a single lesson, but this cure would require the events narrated in the remainder of the Gospel.

Like a thunderbolt, Jesus' rebuke of Peter (16:23) shattered the disciples' euphoria; like a narrow gate into a steep road, his call to martyrdom in verses 24-26 confronted the readers of the Gospel (cp. 7:12f.). The familiarity of modern readers with this story may unduly cushion the shock of these teachings. One is tempted to dwell on Jesus' praise of Peter's faith, in verses 17f., or on his promises of future glory to the disciples, in verses 27-28. But in the original construction of the story the recognition of Jesus' messiahship and sonship had made Peter's dereliction all the more terrible, like that of prophets who kept saying "Lord, Lord" (7:22). In a sense, this is the temptation story of the twelve, corresponding to the temptation story of Jesus (4:1-11). As God's call of Jesus had led immediately to an attack by Satan, so God's revelation to Peter and his choice as the rock had led to a similar attack, which this time had been successful, because Peter and the twelve were still depending on human logic rather than on God's logic. They were not yet ready to use the keys to the kingdom of heaven, for these keys signified the knowledge that the power over Satan had been achieved by death and resurrection (vv. 21, 25). Such an idea would not have been entirely foreign to Matthew's churches, for they were suffering a similar violent persecution (5:10-12, 38-48; chap. 10; 13:1-10; etc.).

The confession in 16:16 was essential to the story, although the major point was not—as many treatments have supposed—the precise titles used by Peter. Similar recognitions had occurred earlier in the Gospel and had been implicit wherever Jesus had become the object of people's reverence. Matthew did not intend to attack as wholly false or misleading the appraisals of the crowds, in verse 14, who confessed that Jesus had exercised an authority as God's prophetic messenger to Israel. Nor did he want to claim that Peter's choice of titles for Jesus must be accepted as normative for the church. Matthew was more interested in the fact that only God had been able to disclose to human beings the truth that this man, who was bound for the cross and whom the authorized interpreters of the scriptures had condemned as demon-possessed, was actually fulfilling his role as God's son (cp. 11:25). What Peter said in verse 22 demonstrated the truth that flesh and blood could not discern in a crucified criminal the "Son of the living God" (v. 16). An even more decisive and amazing point was the promise of Jesus to Peter, in verses 18-19. This promise envisages a continuing struggle between the church— representing the gates of heaven—and "the gates of Hades" (cf. RSV margin), between the powers of life and death, between God and Satan. The keys symbolize victory in this struggle, which was promised to Peter and the church. "Satan cannot unloose what the church binds." As soon as this promise was offered to Peter he fell before the deception of Satan! Astounding, yet no more so than the related promise of the gift of life to followers who are martyred (v. 25), a promise that in verse 28 takes the form of an assurance that they will see the Son of man coming in his kingdom. This vision, like Peter's in verse 17, will be a disclosure not by flesh and blood, but by "my Father."

All later interpreters fail to exhaust the basic meanings of this episode. The original story is as rich in meaning as it is baffling to interpret. No less than a dozen books would be needed to recount the history of interpretation. The chief concern here has been to urge readers to take all sixteen verses as a single unit in Matthew's intention. I believe he wanted to remind the persecuted church of his day that Christ's promise applied to it (16:18, 28). He also wanted to underscore the inescapability of suffering for Jesus, his twelve delegates, and in fact all followers. The story was designed to show the church leaders of his day that their authority, although truly derived from heaven, made them more vulnerable than ever to the temptation of Peter and to the leaven of the Pharisees (v. 11).

The consensus among scholars is that in this story Matthew was dependent on the earlier account in Mark, and that the additions to Mark, found especially in Matthew 16:16b-19, may best be attributed to the Matthean editor. This poses the question of where the editor found this additional material. The answer is: Probably in the traditions telling of the postresurrection appearances of Jesus to Peter. This would make more intelligible the identification of Peter as the rock, the assurance regarding the church, and the transfer of the keys to the kingdom.*

Clearly, the account of the transfiguration (17:1-13) was intended to follow directly the revelation of messianic suffering that had come at Caesarea Philippi. Both disclosures were designed to prepare disciples for events that were to happen soon. In 4:1-11 such a disclosure had initiated the career of Jesus. In 11:25-30 a heavenly revelation of this same order was said to be reflected whenever babes came to trust in the Son of God. In 16:17 Peter's faith in Jesus was traced directly to God's initiative. Now again a mountain vision of heavenly reality is described: Jesus, in garments of heavenly glory, with two representatives of the law and the prophets who had earlier, in popular Jewish lore, been translated to heaven. The vision confirmed the testimony Peter had just given (16:16). However, here, as in the preceding chapter, Peter's inept remark (17:4) reflects the disciple's misunderstanding, ignorance, and perhaps fear, while God's command for Peter to listen to Jesus (v. 5) indicates the way in which Peter's error can be corrected. Verse 9 points ahead to the vocation of the disciples, after Jesus' death and resurrection, to continue Jesus' work. They will then become prophets who relay to God's people their vision of what had been happening in heaven, along with the mandate from God (v. 5). To Matthew, transfiguration and resurrection are mysteries of the same order (cp. 28:16-20) that lie at the heart of the church's existence.

The next episode disclosed the continued impotence of these same men to do their assigned work (17:14-20). Verse 16 expresses the conviction that people were right to bring their sick to the disciples, expecting them to be able to heal. Their failure to do so merited a stinging rebuke from Jesus (v. 17); this failure demonstrated a lack of faith. Jesus was forced to wonder whether enough time remained for him to train them. This "illness" of the disciples attracted far more interest than did the epileptic. Although Matthew telescoped

*Cf. R.E. Brown, *The Gospel According to John* (Garden City, NY: Doubleday, 1970), II, pp. 1088f.

the longer Marcan story into the briefest compass, he retained this accent on the disciples' failure. He also retained Jesus' promise that later these same disciples would receive the required power, once their faith had become as large as a mustard seed. This sequel to the transfiguration story has much the same function as the sequel (16:21-28) to the confession. Both stories would be of greatest relevance to successors of the twelve, leaders of the church who faced the demands of their vocation with all too meager resources.

If there were any doubt about the central theme of all the preceding stories of the Galilean ministry, the announcement of Jesus, in 17:22, should dispel it: "The Son of man is to be delivered...they will kill him." The disciples still did not grasp this. Possibly, Matthew saw the distress of the disciples as something commendable, because it bespoke their love for Jesus. More likely, Matthew wished to stress the fact that the twelve were guilty not only of mistaking Jesus' teaching about suffering (16:21f.), but of refusing to accept his teaching once they understood it. To Matthew, their affection for Jesus may have been as illusory as the duplicity of prophets who said "Lord, Lord" without obeying his command (7:14f.).

What links this duplicity to the next incident (17:24-27), a story Matthew alone has preserved? The men into whose hands the Son of man would be delivered (v. 22) were the temple authorities to whom also the half-shekel tax was paid. The question thus became: Did Jesus support those who later were responsible for his death? The answer would then be fully in line with his instructions in 5:38f. Pay the tax! Not because of fear of the authorities, nor because the law is still binding, but because of the desire not to give offense to the temple authorities. (The danger of giving offense may have attracted this story into the series of teachings that follow [18:6-9].) They must not use their freedom as a means of claiming immunity and privilege. To pay the tax was difficult, because Jesus had no money and had commanded his disciples to give away what they had. This difficulty was met by asking Peter temporarily to return to his erstwhile trade of fishing. The circulation of the story in Matthew's region indicates, according to Gunther Bornkamm, that "the congregation which Matthew represents is still attached to Judaism...(and) in no sense claims for itself exemption from the taxation of the diaspora-congregations."*

A Manual of Discipline (18:1—19:2)

The disciples have been promised the keys of the kingdom (16:16f.). They have been taught, although they have not yet learned, the necessity of suffering for the kingdom. They have served as interns in helping Jesus feed the crowds and heal the sick. Now they must be taught how to govern the church, or how to use the keys. The first of the instructions (18:1-4) provides an authoritative answer to two questions: What requirements for admission to the kingdom should they enforce? By what standard is rank within the kingdom to be determined? A child provided the answer to both. The gate-keeper (a metaphor for a church leader) should admit all who humble themselves. Leaders should also measure rank by the same standard. The ladder of advancement goes down rather than up, which is the opposite of most ladders (23:13). To get the full flavor of this reply, one needs to remember that all Christians, although especially the ordinary folk, were being called children *(paidia)* long before Matthew's day. The use of the term here was probably a conscious pun (Hebrews 2:13-14; 1 John 2:13, 18). Verse 6 defines children as those "who believe in me." (Even more often than children, *little ones* became a term for believers.)

The next teaching (18:5-6) deals directly with dangers faced by leaders in their treatment of weak and insignificant members of their congregations. This teaching gives first the positive command and then the negative warning. (In the later story, in 19:13-15, Jesus exemplifies the positive command, while the twelve illustrate the negative warning.) Every "child" must be welcomed in Christ's name. The Greek word for *receive* was an almost technical word meaning to offer

*Gunther Bornkamm, et al., *Tradition and Interpretation in Matthew* (Philadelphia: Westminster Press, 1963), p. 20.

hospitality as one Christian to another, whereas "in my name" indicates that both the host and the guest are to be understood as representatives of Christ, himself both host and guest in the churches (cp. 10:14, 40-41; Luke 8:21; John 4:45; Galatians 4:14; Hebrews 13:1-3). Because the little ones (ordinary believers) are so dependent on their leaders, the leaders must realize that their own salvation depends on meeting the needs of the least important followers. "The world"—that invisible realm governed by Satan—provides trials from which Christians can never escape, but church leaders can at least avoid becoming the reason why "little ones" lose their faith in Christ (the probable meaning of "cause to sin" in v. 6).

Leaders who think too highly of their own concerns (e.g., feet, hands, or eyes) must begin to fear hell more than they fear being crippled. Those who think too meanly of the "little ones" who have been placed in their care must remember that every such person has immediate access, by way of a guardian angel, to the Father of Jesus. God's mercy is the court where every leader will be immediately accused by any lay person whom he "despises." To support this warning, Matthew uses the parable of the lost sheep (cp. Luke 15:3-7), in which a shepherd talks to subshepherds about the care of sheep that have been led astray. Those who neglect the straying members of the flock directly flout the will of "my Father." (It is probably significant that Matthew has introduced into the parable a word translated "go astray," which elsewhere in the New Testament refers to the divisive influence of false prophets, e.g., Matthew 24:4-5, 11, 24). The salvation of leaders requires their care for the sheep, and especially for those which have apparently left the fold.

Previous sayings deal with basic attitudes of the leaders toward the led, warning against the poisons of "professional" roles within the church. The next set of teachings (18:15-20) provides more specific procedures for handling cases of infraction of the rules. What should the leader do when a brother (a technical term referring either to fellow believer or a fellow teacher) sins against him? The three steps to be followed are outlined with great clarity. First is a direct one-to-one effort to resolve the dispute. Should this fail, two or three should join in trying to resolve the matter. Should this also fail, the whole congregation must be informed and must serve as jury. Should its judgment be rejected, the person would be excluded from the community of believers. Here we see developing the earliest legal procedures for excommunication, procedures designed to protect both the individual and the community. The sinner is guarded against arbitrary and hasty action brought by a single individual or even by two or three leaders. The leader is protected from his own prejudices and from hasty action. The congregation is guarded from violent disruption and from the slow erosion of unresolved antagonisms.

Verses 18f. seem not wholly consistent, because they assign to two or three leaders the final disciplinary action that, in verse 17, had been reserved for the congregation as a whole. The inconsistency probably stems from the fact that these sayings had different origins. Verse 19 appears to be adapted from a general teaching regarding prayer (cp. Matthew 7:7 et al.) that at first applied to all the faithful without exception. Verse 20 was originally an assurance for a wider group facing diverse situations (cp. Matthew 28:20; 11:25-30). Verse 18 stems from the same tradition as 16:16, in which the unique authority of Peter and the twelve was at stake. When these sayings were combined (perhaps attracted to one another by the phrase "two or three" in vv. 16, 19-20) they seemed to deal with the authority of the twelve and their successors for governing the church in ways probably similar to the procedures of Pharisaic scribes in neighboring synagogues.

In the previous teaching, steps had been outlined that would keep disciplinary cases from leading to expulsion or even from reaching congregational adjudication. Now a principle is advanced that would persuade leaders to avoid all such procedures (18:21—19:2). To forgive someone 490 times would postpone disciplinary action against this person indefinitely. This command was reinforced by a parable in which refusal to forgive is seen to bring certain punishment from the lord of forgiveness. Here, as elsewhere in the Gospels, the receiving of divine mercy is made contingent on a person's act of mercy. Discipline within the church thus takes humility (v. 1f.) as the first word and mercy as the last. The threat of divine punishment is addressed to Peter, who significantly appears in every chapter of this section of the Gospel (14:25f.; 15:15; 16:16f.; 17:4, 24f.; 18:21). He stands as spokesman for the twelve, representing their fears, their refusal to accept suffering, their inability to perceive hidden truths, and now their inclination to be less merciful than Jesus. The parable reminds all leaders that any of their "fellow servants" (v. 31) can appeal unmerciful actions to the common Lord and secure redress from him. This is a substantial limitation on the power to bind and loose (16:19; 18:18); whatever binding is to be done by the twelve or their successors must never be allowed to cancel the gift of God's forgiveness. With this parable the manual of discipline preserved the basic radicalism of the prohibition of all judgments (7:1-5) without ignoring the necessity for inflicting occasional penalties within the church.

The editorial conclusion of this manual (19:1-2) is significant on two counts. The shift from Galilee "of the Gentiles" to Judea, stronghold of Jesus' enemies, opens the way for confrontation with these enemies. The healing of the crowds who followed from Galilee suggests that both the training of the twelve and the battles with the Jewish leaders were motivated by Jesus' compassion for the crowds, who now accompanied him to the Holy City, where his death is so soon to follow.

Chapter VII

PREPARATION FOR THE PASSION

The Reversal of Status (19:3—20:28)

Both the crowds and the twelve accompanied Jesus into Judea, although they did not yet comprehend the suffering that awaited him. In this section (19:3-12) the Evangelist combined a teaching for non-disciples with explanations intended for the twelve. Readers should note carefully the specific audience for each saying.

The first audience was the group of Pharisaic scribes who raised a typical scribal problem: how to apply the Mosaic rules on divorce. The scribal question produced a scribal answer for scribes: an appeal to the law concerning the implication of the divine creation of male and female for the sanctity of their union (Genesis 1:27; 2:24). Arguing as a scribe, Jesus interpreted this section of the law (the Pentateuch) as prohibiting divorce. When the scribes called his attention to Moses' provision for divorce (Deuteronomy 24:1-4), Jesus distinguished between the initial purpose of marriage and the later concession given to people because of their hardness of heart. Appealing to God's purpose in creation, he announced that persons who divorced and remarried became adulterers. Whereas Mark permitted no exception, Matthew did permit one—unchastity. Whereas Mark included divorces sought by wives as well as by husbands; not so, Matthew. As addressed to Pharisees and not to disciples, this account may have reflected a desire to show how the scribes had been disloyal to God's purpose in creation, to God's fundamental law.

It is only in the next paragraph (19:10f.) that Jesus addressed the disciples as scribes of the new community. Here the question became an issue not of expediency, but of gift and calling. (This comment in v. 10 discloses the twelve in perhaps their worst light, as men who judged all Jesus' teachings in terms of self-interest.) "Those to whom it is given" should be able to receive and to observe this simple truth, because they "have made themselves eunuchs for the sake of the kingdom of heaven." For them, presumably, sexual desires have been wholly sublimated by their passion for seeking the kingdom of heaven (6:33; 13:44-46). They no longer asked whether divorce was desirable or justified, but what kind of allegiance the kingdom of heaven demanded. Paul was an example of this type of eunuch, although he did not require the same sacrifice from Peter and the other apostles (1 Corinthians 7:1-40; 9:5). The force of this teaching, found only in Matthew, is to impel each leader within the church to ask himself if he is able to receive it, i.e., to live a celibate life because of his vocation. Thus the debate on divorce, provoked by the Pharisees, became a searching test of the disciples' vocation (as outlined in chaps. 10 and 18).

In a succinct form the next episode (19:13-15) provided another case where a situation produced by non-disciples elicited a teaching for disciples. Who brought the children? Probably the crowds of followers, who believed that Jesus, as the Lord, would sanctify these children. Prayer and the laying on of hands had become, in Matthew's day, constitutive features of Christian worship. They were actions expected of leaders, who could bind and loose in Christ's name. So the bringing of children turned the spotlight on the disciples. The moment they rebuked the crowds, they themselves were rebuked by Jesus. For them to despise the children betrayed the gracious character of the kingdom; his action exemplified it. Jesus' healing ministry was thus extended to the children of his followers, a fact also embodied in other stories in which parents interceded for their children (9:18f.; 17:15f.). The coming of the kingdom destroyed any idea of special privilege for any group, old or young, rich or poor, powerful or weak (18:1-5).

It is important to view the next section (19:16-30) as a unit, because the response of Jesus to the rich man became the occasion for a two-pronged dialogue with his disciples, on which Matthew placed a heavy accent. The first paragraph presents a case study in how to respond to rich men who might seek the kingdom (in contrast to children who are brought by their parents). In Matthew's day disciples faced this question: What sort of requirements should be enforced on those who want "eternal life"? Jesus had given a triple answer: obedience to the decalogue, the love of neighbor, and the giving of one's possessions to the poor. Even for a person who accepted the first two requirements, Jesus did not waive the third. Without the third the other two were faulty, if not false. In the end the person excluded himself or herself from the kingdom by refusing its costly requirements (6:19-34). He or she was not willing to become a child again (19:14) or to become last (19:30).

This is an interesting anecdote, but Matthew was more interested in its sequel—a discussion with the disciples that had been prompted by their astonishment over the rigor and inflexibility of Jesus' reply. How can a camel pass through a needle's eye? Surely this rigor made much more difficult the missionaries' work (chap. 10). The protest of the twelve (19:25) was intelligible, although like earlier protests it was intended to show their dullness of hearing. Matthew gave no encouragement to later exegetes who would try to reduce the size of the camel or enlarge the needle's eye. Disciples can either debate what is impossible for human beings or celebrate what God has made possible. When people celebrate God's gift of a new world they will be able to make a total sacrifice for it. Actually, by the time of Matthew there was ample evidence that humans could do the impossible (e.g., 1 Thessalonians 2:9-16; Philippians 3:5-11; 1 Corinthians 1:26-31; Acts 4:34-37). Even so, to require of every convert what Jesus required of this rich man must have made the work of the apostles more difficult.

A second issue raised by this incident was the case of the

twelve themselves, who had made the required sacrifices. To them Jesus gave an amazing set of promises. Their sacrifices would be reimbursed a hundredfold. The goal of eternal life, sought in 19:16, was promised in 19:30 to those who had given up lands, houses, and families. Although this reward was not limited to the twelve (N.B. "every one," in v. 29), they exemplified it and were accordingly assured thrones of glory. Verse 28 suggests the reason for the selection of *twelve* disciples in the first place. Twelve judges were needed to govern the twelve tribes of Israel. This incident clarifies the reasons for Matthew's interest in training these twelve. The whole Gospel was in fact the handbook for this training.*

In the following parable (20:1-16) Jesus continued his discussion with the same disciples concerning the special rewards for their labor. Verse 30 of chapter 19 could stand as an introduction to the parable (N.B. the conjunction "for" in 20:1). Continuity is also shown by the use of similar axioms in 19:30 and 20:16. These clues suggest how Matthew identified the various actors in the parable: the householder to whom the vineyard belongs, and to whose action the kingdom is compared, is Jesus; the laborers represent the twelve and their successors within the church. The contrast among those hired at different hours represents competition among leaders who would begin their vocations at varying times. Viewed from this angle, the parable protests against the idea of special privilege for the first apostles as compared with colleagues and successors. These apostles should not construe the promise of 19:28 in such a way as to guarantee to them superiority over later laborers. This vineyard is no place to feed human pride, no place to measure rewards by merits. Note that Matthew used the same axiom to introduce and to conclude this parable, but he reversed the order. Notice that in 19:30 the accent falls on the second clause, "the last first." In this case the axiom encouraged the twelve (and their successors) to

*Soren Kierkegaard, *Christian Discourses* (London: Oxford University Press, 1940), pp. 184-96.

become last by making a complete sacrifice in line of duty. By contrast, in 20:16, the accent falls on the second clause, "the first last." Thus the axiom becomes a warning to the twelve (and their successors) not to expect special recognition because of their labors. Careful readers will find in verses 13-16 four different punch lines for the same parable, reflecting different accretions during its use in the church. The simplest is probably the best: "Do you begrudge my generosity?"

When we ask what connects the parable to the following situations, two answers emerge: (1) Jesus' central concern for the training of the twelve as those who have been chosen to judge the tribes of Israel (19:28) and (2) the necessity of showing what this enthronement entailed. Disciples still thought about thrones in gentile terms (20:25). This idea had to be destroyed, and it could be destroyed only by the example of the Messiah. He had been enthroned (cp. 28:16 and 20:19) only when he had been condemned by chief priests and scribes, and crucified by gentiles. Herein lay the final clear definition that Jesus had given to royal power and authority. Although all twelve disciples had first misunderstood this new definition, Jesus insisted on repeating the lesson (20:17-19).

Verse 20 introduces an ambitious mother (absent from Mark 10:35), but she quickly disappears from the scene, for in his reply, in verse 22, Jesus addresses the two brothers. In verse 22 Matthew omits the Marcan question regarding baptism, possibly because in his day baptism had become a sacrament for all believers at the beginning of their lives as followers, whereas Matthew was interested here in the special problems to be faced by the twelve and their successors. Moreover, the cup was something that Jesus was about to share with these twelve (26:3-56). To both Matthew and Mark, these verses (20:26-28) represented a genuine climax in the training of the twelve, because they summarized so well what was to happen in Jerusalem and established so clearly an abiding norm for the laborers who should come to work in this vineyard. The story also epitomized many earlier rebukes of the future leaders: "You do not know what you are asking [v. 22]."

The Messianic Demonstration (20:29—21:22)

At this point (20:29) begins the fulfillment of Jesus' declaration: "We are going up to Jerusalem [20:18]." The fact that the crowds have heard this ominous forecast makes all the more striking the number of those "following" on this way. (In Matthew's vocabulary the term may refer simultaneously to the road to Jerusalem, the path of devout pilgrims, and even the Christian community itself.) Herewith the attention ceases to focus on the twelve and shifts to the crowd. When the blind men interrupt his progress, the crowd rebukes them; they quickly learn that Jesus has no tolerance for their exclusiveness. The two blind men are added to the crowd of followers who have been healed through the ready mercy of the Son of David, whose entrance into the city of David elicits such an enthusiastic messianic demonstration. They are sons of David whose eyes have been opened to the Messiah's presence. Their new ability to see becomes a signal both of the blindness of the scribes and of the renewal of the temple (21:14).

Matthew could not think of this entrance into the Holy City in any ordinary terms (21:1-11). This was the arrival of the long-awaited king, coming at last to take up his throne. This event proclaimed to Jerusalem as "daughter of Zion" the coming of her Savior in fulfillment of prophecy (Isaiah 62:11; Zechariah 9:9), a fulfillment the scribes should have recognized. Jesus "staged" his entrance, with the help of his disciples, to dramatize this fulfillment. Such dramatic gestures had long been customary on the part of prophets. The crowds grasped the message: This leader was both Son of David (and therefore messianic king) and a prophet from Nazareth. Their confidence was different from the reaction of the residents of Jerusalem, who at most could ask, "Who is this?" The crowd's enthusiasm was itself a messianic event, for it proclaimed the arrival of the kingdom, with the appropriate signals of welcome, garments spread on the road, and branches cut from trees. To Matthew, the ministry of Jesus had produced a massive upheaval among Jews and gentiles outside

Judea, a widespread public excitement that had cast great fear into the leaders in Judea. Excitement had reached its peak on this occasion in the size of the crowds attending him, in the intensity of their faith, and in the quaking of his opponents. (The verb that is translated *was stirred* was the term usually used for earthquake tremors, 8:24; 24:7; 27:51; 28:2.) In Matthew's day these same conditions were perhaps also characteristic of the course of the Gospel.

The gate into the city led immediately into the temple area, a huge enclosure covering several city blocks, where public events took place. Here teachers gathered to conduct their schools. Much business was transacted, especially the sale of animals or birds for sacrifice. On this occasion (21:12-17), although many things must have transpired, only four things are reported: (1) Jesus' prophetic action to reclaim "my house"; (2) the continuation of his ministry of healing; (3) the messianic shouts of the crowds; (4) the anger of the priests and scribes. These were the essential elements in the wider drama, now being staged in the holiest place. Matthew was convinced that each of these developments fulfilled prophecy (cf. Isaiah 56:7; Jeremiah 7:11; Psalm 8:2). The word children referred to the entire company of Jesus' followers (cf. v. 9) but made more obvious the connection between the prophecy and the members of the church. The "house" that robbers had desecrated belonged to God but also to Jesus, who claimed it as his own. The praise due to him on this occasion was now being "perfected," but by strangers in the den of robbers, for the scribes and priests had stolen from God the praise due to God. Children from Galilee restored the house to its proper use. The prompt withdrawal of Jesus from the temple and from the city may also have been intended as a prophetic gesture, a shaking of the dust off his feet as a witness against a house that had not received him (cp. 10:14; 15:21; 24:1).

The story of the fig tree (21:18-22) has tantalized interpreters from the beginning. What happened? What did it mean? Taken literally, it is unlike other actions reported about Jesus; in this case it reads like a bit of pious legend that celebrates Jesus' power over nature. If not taken literally, what is its symbolic value? This fig tree bristles with thorns for the interpreter. Matthew has eased the problem by omitting the Marcan comment that it was not the season for ripe figs. He also eased the problem by making it clear that the story was told for the sake of teaching the disciples something about the power of faith. The context provides further clues. This story described the occasion when the Son of David, on visiting the center of Israel, had found God's house turned into the stronghold of his enemies. Because Israel had at times been spoken of as a fig tree, the desire of the Messiah for fruit from this tree becomes entirely intelligible, as does the fact that the tree now had no fruit (cp. 21:34). Granted that his visits to the city and the temple often produced prophetic gestures on his part, this cursing of the tree could be taken as a prophetic gesture or at least as a parable against rebellious Israel (cp. Luke 13:6-9), even though the story has now lost its parabolic beginning: "There was a man who planted a fig tree..." This story could then be a Judean equivalent for the "woes" that Jesus had uttered against the unrepentant cities in Galilee (11:20-24). Jerusalem was denounced as the bad tree that cannot bear good fruit (7:18f.). The fruitless fig tree probably represented to Matthew the hostility toward the church on the part of the religious authorities in Israel, a hostility which Jesus had defeated and which in later decades his delegates could overcome by their faith.

Confrontation in the Temple (21:23—24:2)

"My house" has become a den of robbers (21:13). The stories of Jesus' debates in this house give the historical details of the struggle between owner and thieves. The accounts begin with the promise that by faith the disciples can move the mountain of massive antagonism; they end with the same promise couched in different imagery: The awesome walls of the temple, center of enmity, would be reduced to rubble (24:2). Between this beginning and this end comes a series of debates.

In the first debate (21:23-27) Jesus dealt with the issue

of authority. The controversy was initiated by the chief priests and elders, who represented the highest ecclesiastical power of the day. The temple was the logical place for this collision, because it was both the center of their power and the goal of the messianic work. So, too, the issue of authority was the nub of the matter, and on this issue Jesus' reply followed three lines. In the first he placed the antagonists on the defensive by asking whether, in their judgment, John had spoken and acted with divine or human credentials. To avoid a trap, they refused to answer. This paradigm invites several inferences: The crowd of Jesus' attendants from Galilee had fully accepted John's baptism as authorized by God (cp. 11:7-15); John had from the first disclosed the duplicity of the rulers from Jerusalem (3:7-12); that duplicity now became evident in their refusal to answer Jesus' question (21:27).

Jesus' second line of argument was embodied in the parable of the two sons, a trap into which the rulers fell by answering the trigger question (21:28-32). This enabled Jesus to identify the obedient son with the tax collectors and harlots, those political traitors and religious outcasts, and to identify Jesus' opponents with the dishonest and disobedient son. They had not accepted John as accredited messenger from God and had been repelled by the disreputable folk who had followed John. Yet John's authority had in fact come from God. Jesus thus associated himself, John, and their followers in this great controversy between God and the rulers of Israel.

A third trap was set by telling an elaborate allegory (21:33-46) of a farmer and his vineyard. Here the trigger was the question in verse 40. By answering it (v. 41) the priests and elders pronounced a horrible verdict on themselves. Jesus had told the story in such a way as to implicate them: They were the tenants to whom the householder (God) had rented the vineyard (Israel). It was they who had violently refused to grant the owner's share to his agents (the prophets, wise men, scribes, John the Baptist). The climax of their agelong sins had come with their treatment of the owner's son and heir, Jesus (vv. 37-39). In fulfillment of the prophecy of Psalm 118:22f. this son had been made the cornerstone of the new temple (or possibly the keystone in its central arch). On their part they had forfeited the vineyard to a nation that would produce fruit for its owner (unlike the fig tree in 21:19). This allegory is perhaps the strongest evidence that Matthew lived in a region where churches had finally broken off all contact with the synagogues. We may safely assume that Christian scribes often used this allegory to defend the church's gentile mission against their Jewish neighbors, whether or not these neighbors were, as W.D. Davies argues, the famous rabbinic school at Jamnia.*

Another allegory, which Matthew probably had found in another source (cf. Luke 14:15-24), conveys a similar threat (22:1-14). Its effectiveness as a trap is lessened because it is so unlikely an account of a wedding. (Who would kill those who bring such invitations? Or burn down the city of those who refuse them?) The king obviously represents God, who has prepared a wedding feast (a popular metaphor for the messianic kingdom) for his son and who invites guests to come to the feast. We may note several points of contrast with the previous allegory. The conception of *guests* focuses attention less sharply on religious leaders and more clearly on the response of Israel as a whole, set over against the response of the gentiles. The incident of the king sending his troops to burn the city (v. 7) may echo the Roman destruction of Jerusalem in the war of A.D. 66 to 70, yet it is difficult to attribute to Christian teachers the notion that these Roman troops had belonged to God, who used them as agents to kill the murderers of God's son by burning Jerusalem. This would indeed be a strange act to assign to a God of mercy (5:38-48). The most significant new element appears at the end (vv. 11-14). Because both bad and good have been included in the new guest list (v. 10; cp. 13:24f., 47f.) the king must scrutinize all guests and exclude those not properly dressed for the occasion. In these verses the allegory ceases to protest against Pharisaic opposition and becomes a warning against the

*The Setting of the Sermon on the Mount (New York: Cambridge University Press, 1964), pp. 256-315.

113

"many" who have accepted the invitation. From the perspective of the Evangelist, these would represent Christians who, after conversion, become unwilling to pay the costs of wedding garments, i.e., they refuse to wear clothes that have been made white by the endurance of suffering (Revelation 3:4, 18).

Having stumbled clumsily into Jesus' traps, the Pharisees now set their own trap for Jesus (22:15-22). They enlisted two groups: the Herodians, who as supporters of the government would report to the political rulers any trace of sedition, and their own students, whom they had trained to apply the scripture to practical matters. These student rabbis praised Jesus as one who had given full priority to God's will over desires for popularity. Then they asked a question so constructed that any answer, whether positive or negative, would incriminate him. A *yes* would betray the first commandment, a *no* would make him guilty of sedition. By his reply Jesus forced them, as students of the law, to decide for themselves where to draw the line between God's jurisdiction and Caesar's. Although the church then, as later, found this reply eminently useful, the saying has never been sufficient by itself to solve the whole range of problems posed in political ethics. The riddle remains that each must solve for himself or herself. Keep in mind that the first audience for this riddle was neither the crowd nor the disciples, but only their adversaries.

Only in the next episode does Matthew recount a direct confrontation between Jesus and the Sadducees alone (22:23-33). Elsewhere they are associated with the Pharisees (3:7; 16:1, 6, 11-12), and the latter always take the more prominent role. Composed mainly of priestly families whose professional careers were dependent on the temple, the party of the Sadducees fell into oblivion after the temple's destruction in A.D. 70 and ceased to be a real obstacle to the work of the church. Curiously, their denial of the resurrection also brought them on stage at the time of Paul's trial (Acts 23:6f.). Because of their refusal to believe in life after death they enjoyed debating with the Pharisees over various dilemmas that belief in a future life entails. The case they put to Jesus is typical of these dilemmas. It presupposed the procedures stipulated in the Mosaic law (Deuteronomy 25:5). If a childless husband died, his wifeless brother would inherit the duty of marrying the widow. Assuming that seven brothers had, in obedience to Moses, married the same woman, whose wife would she be in the afterlife? Jesus called his questioners wrong on two counts. If they had known the scriptures and the power of God, they would have known that God is God of the living. Furthermore, if they had trusted in this God and not in plausible answers to skeptical conundrums, they would have realized that life in heaven would be vastly different from life on earth. Presumably, this answer temporarily silenced his adversaries; perhaps it was never intended to do much more.

In the next two episodes (22:34-46) the confrontation in the temple reached its climax. This climax covered the two major points at issue—the law and the Messiah. On the first issue the question raised by the Pharisees enabled Jesus to announce from the temple his basic convictions concerning the two chief commandments. By implication Matthew wanted Christian teachers of his day to use this answer against their adversaries in the synagogue, and he wanted the churches to observe this summary of all legal obligations (cp. 5:17-20; 7:12).* In their question the scribes followed a practice common to the rabbis, who often sought to condense all regulations to a few essentials; in his answer Jesus arrived at virtual agreement with some of the rabbis.

Jesus took the initiative in posing the issue of messiahship. With this subject the scribes were expected to be familiar. Whose son was the Messiah to be? The question is placed in a most dramatic setting, where the debates have reflected great hostility toward Jesus and where Jesus is about to command his disciples and other followers not to imitate these scribes. The scribes gave a ready answer: The Messiah will be the Son of David. To this answer Jesus objected, basing his objection on a psalm that had been widely used in both synagogue and church as a messianic declaration (Psalm 110:1;

*Soren Kierkegaard, *Works of Love* (Princeton, NJ: Princeton University Press, 1946), pp. 15-109.

Acts 2:34-35; Hebrews 1:13; 10:13). The full reasons for this objection are not certain. It is improbable that sonship to David was being denied (cf. 1:1; 9:27; 12:3, 23; 15:22; 20:30; 21:9, 15) but probable that sonship *to God* is being tacitly affirmed. Perhaps a contrast is being drawn between David, who called the Christ "Lord," and the Pharisees, who fail to do so. Perhaps the Pharisees are being viewed as the "enemies" who must be subjugated by the Messiah. At any rate the enthronement of Jesus at the right hand of God is here announced in the house of David as a fulfillment of the promise to David; this enthronement is understood to explain both the crowds' hosannas at the entry (21:9, 15) and the later exaltation of Jesus (28:16).

For several chapters now the Evangelist has been giving his account of the long and bitter debates between Jesus and his opponents. With 23:1 the audience shifts from the scribes to the crowd and to the disciples. Presumably, the disciples have been present all along in the temple. Moreover, in contrast to other major addresses of Jesus, here the two groups share the stage. After 23:13 the Pharisees return to the stage but primarily as an object lesson on what Jesus' followers must avoid at all costs, both leaders and laypersons.

When this series of warnings is first read it seems to apply primarily to the disciples rather than to the crowds, or in terms of the later churches, to leaders rather than to laypersons. Christian leaders followed a vocation similar to that of the rabbis, As leaders, they could easily load others with burdens (cp. 16:18; 18:20) they would themselves refuse to carry. They could crave titles commensurate with their status: rabbi, father, master. These ambitions, common to leaders, were ruled out by Jesus' standard of greatness (23:11; cp. 20:26). The basic intention in all these teachings was to undercut the pride and pretensions of Christian teachers; laypersons were not so strongly tempted to mimic the Pharisees.

Yet the crowds (lay folk) were also involved. If leaders are inclined to seek honor, success in these efforts depends on the ordinary membership. "Call no man your father" is addressed to followers who are tempted by flattery to seek favors for themselves. Moreover, the first of the commands applies especially to the "common" believer. "Practice... whatever they tell you [23:3]." Antagonism against synagogue teachers should not induce Christians to scorn the law. The law must be honored (cp. 5:20), even though professional interpreters of the law be repudiated.

This paragraph, then, is not so anti-Semitic as it may sound. The target of the teaching is not Israel as a whole, inasmuch as both the crowds and the disciples also belong to Israel. The attack is limited to synagogue teachers, and the purpose of the attack was not so much to arouse hatred of them as to warn Christian teachers against similar professional poisons. What is said about the Pharisees makes all the more horrible the dangers of hypocrisy among Christ's servants (e.g., 24:51).

The series of seven woes (23:13-33) comes as the climax to the confrontation between the Messiah and the leaders of Israel in the temple. It matches the series of beatitudes given to members of Israel who exemplified the opposite traits (5:3-12). *Hypocrites*, used six times, is a condemnation based on the gap between their claims and their behavior. Five times they are dubbed blind, a trait especially dangerous for those who wish to serve as guides (cp. 15:14). This epithet strikes a sharp contrast, probably intentional, to the many blind men in the Gospel who, on believing, are healed and join the crowd of followers (9:27; 11:5; 12:22; 15:30; 20:30), even within the temple itself (21:14). All seven woes are illustrations of the basic treachery indicated in verse 3: These religious authorities in Israel do not practice the law of which they are interpreters and guardians. This means that instead of helping people to enter the kingdom they discourage them (v. 13). Because of their malfeasance their keys have now been given to the twelve (16:19; 18:18). As teachers, they bear responsibility for the damnation of their pupils, a principle Jesus earlier applied to the twelve (18:7-10). These blind fools have allowed themselves to be deceived by their own casuistry (cp. 23:16-22 with 5:33-37), committing monstrous sins in the effort to avoid trivial errors. They have forgotten that inward desires are the only source of outward cleanness (cp. 23:25-26 with 15:1-20). To feel the stunning force of the fifth and sixth woes (23:25-28), one must recall the painstaking efforts with which the scribes, in fulfillment of the law, sought to avoid all ceremonial defilement, and the degree to which burial tombs had become a symbol of maximum defilement. To call them, of all people, whitewashed tombs was the acme of insult. So, too, the seventh woe touched them at a sensitive spot, for they were highly respected as guardians of the monuments built to honor heroes and martyrs. What challenge could be greater? Where could this challenge be offered more provocatively than in the temple? To themselves they were sons of the prophets, but to Jesus, sons of those who had murdered the prophets. More than this, Jesus announced that he would send prophets, wise men, and scribes into their midst, a direct reference to the period between his death and Matthew's day. The fate of these messengers seals the verdict against the synagogue leaders (23:34-36). To return to the key defection: As Matthew saw it, the ultimate cleavage between Jesus and the Pharisees was occasioned by their variant interpretations of the law. Synagogue rulers ignored the triple demand for justice, mercy, and faith (v. 23). Jesus and, on his instructions, later leaders of the church were bound to consider these three ideals as the final test of obedience to God. This trilogy is fully comparable to the famous trilogy of Paul (1 Corinthians 13:13) or of Micah (6:8).

Notice two things at the conclusion of his attack. Jesus foresaw the death of his own representatives, and yet he commissioned them to go into the heartland of this enemy. Why? *"Therefore* I send you" (23:34). The hostility of the Pharisees here becomes the very reason for the Christian mission to Israel and even to the Pharisees. This announcement recalls the passages in which Jesus, in an apparent display of parochial nationalism, limits to the cities of Israel his own mission (15:24) and that of the twelve (10:5-6). From this passage one infers that it may have been the very treason of the synagogue leadership which induced Jesus to insist on the work within Israel.

To Jesus (and to Matthew?) this mission by the church to Israel need not be supported by the expectation of success. It could serve to fill up the measure of rebellion, to complete the sad epoch of anti-God activity on the part of pro-God forces. One might find in 23:35-36 a measure of unholy gloating over the destruction of these enemies were it not for the sequel (vv. 37-39), where the dominant notes are the love of the Messiah for this city, his grief over its blindness, and his undiminished desire for its salvation.

Nothing could be more fitting to end the confrontation in the temple than the prophetic gesture of the Messiah's withdrawal: "Jesus left the temple [24:1]." Nor is it surprising that his followers should be overwhelmed by the strength of the opposition which these ancient and massive buildings symbolized. How could they overcome such intrenched resistance? In response to such a contrast between power and weakness Jesus predicted the total destruction of this holiest place (24:2).

If we are correct in our analysis, the Evangelist, in arranging the traditions used in chapters 19 to 23, was concerned with both the past and the future as seen from his own time. In connection with the past, he wished to clarify the developing animosity between Jesus and the Jewish leaders that led directly to the Passion story. This animosity he explained in terms of clashing views of authority and different views on how Israel should fulfill its vocation as God's people (the three parables in 21:28—22:10 are keys). Because all Jesus' debates with the Jews remained current in Matthew's church, these debates are interspersed with "lessons" for the disciples (e.g., 19:23—20:28). Both debates and lessons had value for Matthew's churches, because many of their members were Jews (23:3) who were constantly engaged in the difficult and dangerous mission. "I send you prophets [23:34]" applied to them in their work among synagogues whose leaders had not recognized John and Jesus as prophets (21:23-32).

Matthew was also greatly interested in the future of the mission on the part of this new Israel composed of tax collectors and harlots (21:32) and of wedding guests "both bad and good" who had been gathered from the streets (22:10). This community knew what sufferings Jesus had endured— psychic and physical—and knew that he had predicted the same fate for them (23:34). They could endure such deaths only if they had from Jesus some answers to the questions of 24:3. In chapters 24 and 25 Matthew devotes himself almost exclusively to these answers.

The Messiah's prediction here is an alternative way of saying what he had said in 23:33 or 23:36 or 23:38. The house was left desolate both by the Messiah's departure from it (not to return before a national repentance) and by its impotence to defeat God's mysterious designs with regard to this very nation (1:22-23).

A Manual of Signs (24:3—25:46)

Matthew made clear to his readers the strategic location of the last of the five "sermons." Like the first, it was given on a mountain, symbolic of divine revelation. This mountain was the Mount of Olives, east of the temple area, overlooking the place of his recent confrontation with the Pharisees. Limiting his teaching to the twelve, he could now devote himself to preparing them for the Passion, revealing things not disclosed to others (cf. 13:16-17). The connections with the preceding chapter are elusive but important. The seven woes had prompted baffling predictions concerning the close of the time of rebellion and the destruction of the temple. Among the chief sins of the Pharisees had been their desire for signs (12:38f.; 16:1f.), a desire Jesus had peremptorily refused to gratify. Now his own disciples asked for signs. The whole of these two chapters may be taken as an answer, although it actually is a collection of many different materials that had originated at different times and for different purposes. Matthew is responsible for the organization and editing of this material, even though in chapter 24 he follows Mark rather closely and in chapter 25 some of the parables may have come to him through Q.

Jesus' first response to the demand for signs is to discourage it. He sharply warns that any excitement over catastrophic signs can easily deceive his followers. There will be impressive movements within the church that falsely announce his coming. There will be wars, famines, and earthquakes, but such events should not be construed as signs of the end. Those who followed prophets who capitalized on such omens would be led astray. One mark of the false prophet (the twelve are, of course, viewed as true prophets) would be to appeal to such catastrophes as omens of the Messiah's coming, either in the wilderness or in some secret rendezvous within the city. This kind of excitement over the end of the world must be rejected; his own coming could be predicted no more than people can tell in advance where and when a bolt of lightning may strike (24:23-28).

Nor should church leaders be deceived by disturbances within the church. They can expect persecution and martyrdom; they will find Christians defecting, betraying, hating; it may seem that the final failure of good and the triumph of evil is at hand. Yet they should not read such dire portents as signs of the end. The twelve should allow nothing to distract them from the assignment to which Jesus has called them (24:14; cp. 10:7-23; 28:16-20). This was a direct, if also noncommittal, answer to the query of verse 3. Yet such an answer did not satisfy the leadership of the church, partly because, as interpreters of the Old Testament, they could not so readily dismiss the predictions found there, and partly because the traditions within the church provided other views which, as teachers, they felt obliged to preserve. Moreover, they could not easily quell the innate human desire to anticipate the end; they were not satisfied with the command to keep on with their work (v. 14).

Although Jesus continued to warn against premature excitements, we find also a collection of various teachings concerning cosmic repercussions of the coming of the Son of man (24:15-31). The coming of the Son of man, itself a great sign (v. 30), will be preceded by cosmic earthquakes that will disturb the heavenly bodies. These earthquakes will in turn be preceded by the great tribulation—a period shorter than originally intended yet a definite period of agony—at the outbreak of which people are ordered to flee to the mountains. This flight will be triggered by the appearance of Daniel's "desolating sacrilege," a reference the reader is enjoined to understand but which leaves most readers more puzzled than ever. In passages like this it may be wisest simply to confess ignorance. If Jesus so instructed his disciples, it is impossible now to recover what he meant. If Matthew discerned a special message here for his readers (the teaching successors of the twelve), the message is no longer readily accessible to us. In any case it is doubtful if we can translate these signs into equivalent events in modern history.

The previous teachings seem to be motivated by the disciples' desire to know in advance when the Son of man would come. This seems also to be the purpose of the analogy of the fig tree (24:32-44). When "these things" (the antecedent is unclear) take place, and not until then, one can know the end is at hand. Yet this purpose collides with the plain truth of verse 42 (one cannot know the time in advance) and of verse 44 (the day will be unexpected). The reference to Noah stresses this suddenness and unexpectedness. The processes of judgment cannot be anticipated, for no one knows the day. If this is true, it would seem to follow that all seeking of signs is futile and wrong. The Noah analogy seems to cancel out the answers of verses 15 to 31 and to teach that every person must be ready every day. "Watch—not for signs but for the Son of man. Be ready for his coming" (v. 42). In earlier chapters the Evangelist expressed the double conviction: The Son of man has appeared in fulfillment of scripture, yet no one had known in advance how such fulfillment would take place. As Jesus now prepares the disciples for the period after his death, a similar theme emerges: The end will come in fulfillment of Jesus' own promises, but no one can know in advance the time and place. There will be no way of reducing the uncertainties, no substitute for constant readiness.

The discussion concerning the signs does not end at 24:44, for Jesus continues his address to the same audience, without a break and without any other question from his disciples (24:45—25:13). To be sure, a question appears in verse 45, but it is posed by the teacher himself. The disciples should have asked it in 24:3, but they had raised instead the question that is so often used to lead people astray by enabling them to anticipate the future. Disciples should have asked how to fulfill their assignment, how to be faithful and wise, how to watch. To this question Matthew provided an answer consisting of a collection of four parables, drawn from Mark, Q, and a special source. All four deal with the return of a master to his servants at an unexpected time and in unexpected ways. The injunction to be ready would be a fitting conclusion to all four (24:44; 25:13). In traditional eschatological imagery these parables depict ways in which faithful servants will be separated in the final judgment from the unfaithful. In all four, readers can readily identify one figure with Jesus and the others with his disciples. Just as his opening sermon had reached a climax in a warning to the disciples against self-deceived treachery (7:15f.), so his valedictory sermon, delivered on the Mount of Olives immediately before the Passion, concluded with the same warning, repeated in four stories, each of which ended with a curse on his followers who later would become hypocrites.

The first parable defines watchfulness in terms of dependability in feeding the Lord's household (24:45-51). The true deacon never feeds himself first, never uses his energies in fighting with his fellow deacons. Preparation for the return of the Lord is wholly defined by unselfish behavior toward colleagues among the leaders and "little ones" among the members. It is logical that, for leaders guilty of brutality, the final verdict of the Lord should come suddenly and devastatingly, and that the remorse over their pious self-deception should be total. Here it becomes apparent that wickedness and hypocrisy are not so much flagrant and conscious misdeeds as self-deception that produces complacency about one's loyalty to the master.

The second parable (25:1-12) does not define so clearly what specific actions serve to put disciples in the position of the five sleeping maidens who were caught unprepared. Evidently, they have had a specially favored relation to the bride-groom and they unwisely continue to rely on his favor. This favor makes the verdict all the more shocking to them (v. 12). Yet for a definition of what was the sin of the sleeping maidens one must rely either on the previous parable or on typical early Christian attitudes toward sleep. One thinks, for example, of the Gethsemane scene (26:40ff.) or the Pauline teaching (1 Thessalonians 5:6ff.; Ephesians 5:14) or the parable of the tares (Matthew 13:25). Perhaps for Matthew sleeping connoted disobedience to the specific commands in the Sermon on the Mount. In the final accounting the disciples will be judged by this standard (cp. 25:12 with 7:21-27). The parable makes clear that they deserve the Lord's exclusion, and that his closing of the door surprises them. They had relied too much on his goodwill and not enough on their own obligations.

The parable of the talents (25:14-30), like that of the wedding feast, fails to define the kind of action which would effectively prepare servants for the master's return. To be sure, it does not encourage the usual interpretation which, identifying talent with every individual's inborn capacities (e.g., a special aptitude for music), assumes that the faithful servant is any person who makes the most of native abilities during his or her adult career. This parable thinks rather in terms of those special gifts conveyed to leaders of a Christian community that obligate them to serve as stewards of a particular master and to render an accounting to him (like the charismata of 1 Corinthians 12). This parable focuses on the specific sin of the one-talent man who, despite the Lord's trust, chooses to be unproductive. What his failure was remains dubious. Was he one of the laborers sent into the vineyard, in 9:37ff., who objected because the work was too difficult, or because the harvest belonged to an absentee owner? Was he, as a Christian teacher, guilty of the earlier treason of the scribes, in 21:35, who claimed for themselves the yield from their own labor? We do not know. The safer clue is to interpret the less certain by the more certain, i.e., to interpret this parable by its sequel.

The parable of the final judgment (25:31-46) gives a transparent answer concerning the kind of behavior desired by the King. The speaker is Jesus; the audience, the twelve—with their special assignments; the time of instruction, the close of their training, immediately before the death of the teacher. The time for which the instruction is given is the period after Jesus' death and before the anticipated coming of the Son of man (v. 31). The imagined scene of the parable is the judgment he will execute. (Readers should remember that everything here, including the depiction of final judgment, is given in parabolic, not scientific, language.) There are four sets of characters: (1) the king-judge, who acts for his Father; (2) the least of these, his brothers, who are hungry, thirsty, naked, sick, and imprisoned; (3) the blessed; (4) the accursed. The identification of these is beyond doubt: (1) Jesus; (2) members of the church and especially "the least of these," who during his absence represent him; (3) teachers, judges, exorcists, deacons within the church who by their faithfulness become heirs of the kingdom; (4) leaders who have defaulted on their duties to the "little ones" (cp. 18:5-11), unaware that in them Jesus was present incognito. (This analysis allots no separate role to the "nations" of v. 32. The category does not recur and seems alien to Matthew's purpose. It may have been present in a pre-Matthew version, where there was less concern for the duties of leaders.)

The Gospel was written when churches were living in the midst of harsh political, religious, social, and economic conditions in which many of "the least of these" were starving or in prison. It was hazardous for leaders of the churches to visit such prisoners and minister to their basic needs (cp. 5:3-10, which we interpreted as applying to laypersons, and 5:11-12, as addressed to leaders). The parable suggests the unexpectedness and the finality with which Jesus' blessing and curse would be exercised in the midst of these conditions. Those leaders who assumed the Lord had delayed his return (24:48) could not have been more mistaken. They had deceived themselves but had not deceived him with regard to their faithfulness. (Cp. the essay on this parable in Supplement 4.)

By placing this allegory last in the series, Matthew probably wanted to indicate that it provides the best answer both to the inept question of the disciples concerning the end of the age (24:3) and to his own more astute question, in 24:45, concerning the measure of a disciple's wisdom. In fact, when a student reads the earlier, more baffling discussion of signs in the light of 25:31-46, some of the riddles become less baffling (e.g., 24:21f., 26, 38, 40f.).

Chapter VIII

COVENANT AND MANDATE

When he had completed the fifth major sermon, Matthew took up from Mark the story of the Passion. Several distinctive things should be noted about this story:

1. It is a single connected story, with the various episodes linked together so tightly that none can be understood by itself.

2. The individual actors are clearly identified by name, so that the role of each becomes distinct and continuous. Even though the accounts of Judas and Peter are broken up into several separate scenes, the action of each apostle is sharply etched.

3. In contrast with earlier parts of the Gospel, here the reader has been prepared for the story. Verse 2 in chapter 26—which is the prelude to almost everything that happens—harks back to several earlier warnings and announcements. In fact the last paragraph (28:16-20) is the genuine consummation of the entire Gospel. One can stop reading at 28:20 with the feeling that nothing essential has been omitted; this would not have been so if one had stopped earlier. The interpretation of the earlier chapters in Matthew is enhanced if one keeps this story in mind.

4. The account is so authentic as a story that its message cannot be translated into a non-story form. Its meaning is embodied in what happened. Many teachers might have been tempted to reduce the story to its dogmatic or moral gist, but not so Matthew. The narrative unfolds in such a way that the

narrator does not intrude into it. On the contrary, everyone becomes a listener, sharing in the dramatic momentum of events.

The Passover Covenant (26:1-56)

The opening verse (26:1) resembles the conclusion of the four earlier sermons (7:28; 11:1; 13:53; 19:1), except for the inclusion of the word *all;* Jesus' formal instruction is over. The next verse reminds readers of earlier predictions (especially 16:21f.; 17:12, 22f.; 20:18; 21:38f.) that now are to be fulfilled. The time is highly significant, because the Passover was the holiest day in the sacred calendar. For Jesus to be delivered up on the Passover (measured in Jewish fashion from sunset to sunset) meant that his crucifixion would be forever linked to the exodus of Israel from Egypt. The use of the word deliver is especially weighty; it appears as a way of describing the betrayal by Judas (26:15-16, 21, 23-25, 45-46, 48), the official procedures of the priests (27:2, 18), and the final command of Pilate (27:26). In using the same word, the story implicates many people in guilt, all the while it preserves the conviction that Jesus knew and accepted in advance all that happened.

Caiaphas was high priest from A.D. 18 to 36; this fact sets outside limits for the date of the crucifixion. The plan to arrest Jesus supports what Matthew's account as a whole has said, that Jesus had attracted so large a following, especially of Galileans, that the rulers were alarmed. There is an apparent contradiction between the plot ("not during the feast") and the fact that Jesus was arrested during the feast. Perhaps the adversaries wanted an arrest "by stealth," hidden from the festival throngs in the temple. Why was Judas needed by the priests? To identify Jesus to those who might otherwise not recognize him, especially at night? To give testimony against Jesus at the trial? To guide the captors to the place where Jesus spent the night, so that they could capture him quietly? Matthew does not provide precise answers; he leaves similarly vague the motives of Judas. Desire for money may well have been a factor, even though the note concerning the bribe may have been suggested by the prophecy in Zechariah 11:12, a prophecy that helped to shape other details in the Passion story.

The anointing (26:6-13) illustrates one feature of the Passion story: its tendency to present black and white contrasts. The hospitality of Simon the leper stands over against the caution of Simon Peter. The indignation of the disciples (26:8) is rebuked by the prophetic foresight of an anonymous woman. More clearly, the generosity of this woman in wasting an expensive perfume provides a silent condemnation of the greed of Judas. Accordingly, the memory of her deed will last as long as the message of the world's salvation (v. 13). In this context the saying about the poor should not be taken as a teaching on poverty, but simply as a pointed reminder of Jesus' death and of the appropriateness of acts of love and adoration.

The account of the Passover supper (26:17-29) stressed the certainty of the death of Jesus and its nearness. The arrangement for the room was occasioned by the declaration, "My time is at hand." During the supper the first item of conversation was the prophecy of betrayal, along with the recognition of the necessity of the death itself. The words interpreting the bread and the wine were focused on the death. The meal was explicitly designated as the last meal of Jesus with his disciples until they would be reunited in the kingdom.

One of the essential features of the story is the role of the disciples:

1. They prepared for the meal in accordance with the Master's instructions. This story probably reflects the custom in Matthew's churches.

2. They joined in the discussion concerning betrayal, a discussion that expressed both terrible guilt and intense sorrow. Later celebrations of the eucharist would embody both emotions.

3. They ate the bread and drank the wine.

All were included within the terms of this covenant, in which their betrayals would be bracketed within the forgiveness of sins. Moreover, this covenant not only dealt with their sins; it promised a new feasting "with you" in the Father's kingdom (cp. 19:28). Presumably, this account of the Last Supper became the model the twelve followed after Jesus' death, as they sought to obey his command to feed the multitudes left under their care (14:19; 15:36; 24:45).

As an inset within the larger story of the Passion, the account of the supper conveyed much of the significance of the larger story. It enabled the church to reenact the events that belonged to "this Gospel." The correspondence between these events and the churches' worship is clearer than in either of the other Synoptics. As a scribe writing a manual for other scribes, Matthew felt an obligation to provide materials adapted to liturgical needs.* Unlike modern churches, which use a short reading of scripture in eucharistic celebrations, Matthew's churches probably listened to a reading of the Passion story as a whole. In interpreting these chapters we should remember this sacramental context.

The hymn sung at the supper table (26:30) was probably drawn from the Hallel psalms (Psalm 130-148). The Mount of Olives had been the site of Jesus' last address, possibly carrying on the chain of significant mountain scenes in Matthew. The story of this address should not be separated from the supper, as the action continues without a break within the context of the Passover celebration. Here, as earlier, the conversation proceeds between Jesus and "all the disciples" (vv. 27, 31). Peter's assertion that he is exempt from the others' weakness is disallowed (vv. 33, 35).

Each episode in the dramatic action conveys a prophecy of later episodes; in this case the prophecies are fulfilled quickly—for example, Jesus' warning of their scattering and his assurance of going to Galilee—the warning was fulfilled that very night, the assurance a short time later. Matthew follows Mark in showing a special interest in the rendezvous in Galilee, because it is only there that the risen Lord appears

*Cf. G.D. Kilpatrick, *The Origins of the Gospel of St. Matthew* (Oxford: Clarendon Press, 1946), pp. 67-100.

(unlike the accounts in Luke). In this respect Matthew may simply have been following the Marcan tradition. However, his churches may have been more closely related to Galilee. Or he may have wanted to associate the Gospel more closely with the gentile mission (4:15), perhaps to protest against domination by Jewish-Christian leaders in Judea.

Jesus' warning, in which he announced a scattering before this final gathering, constituted a sad climax to all the earlier scenes in which disciples had a part. They were not yet ready, despite the plain word of Zechariah 13:7 and Jesus' own earlier warnings, for their shepherd to be struck down. They were not yet able, despite Peter's protestations, to die with him (a clear echo of the rule that every follower must lose his life [16:25]). Proof of this unreadiness was provided by their flight (26:56), as well as by the later cowardice of Peter (v. 75). These failures were symbolized by their inability to watch (the Gethsemane account indicates graphically the central meaning of the command in 24:42). The weakness of the flesh (v. 41) made them vulnerable to the attack by Satan, when they realized that the cost of faithfulness would be their own deaths. This shows why people (including the chief disciples) needed to pray, "Deliver us from the Evil One" (6:13). Irony is conveyed by the disclosure that the battle had been lost while the disciples were sleeping (sleep was a basic Christian term for infidelity), whereas the battle of Jesus was being won at that very moment. The trial Jesus faced was the sort of trial by Satan from which the church needed to be delivered. Gethsemane rather than Golgotha was the place where Jesus won his own personal struggle with Satan.

Matthew's assurance that Jesus had come to fulfill the law and the prophets (5:17) was based in part on events like the arrest of Jesus (26:47-56). The arrest was made by a crowd delegated by the chief priests and elders of "the people" (God's covenant people, Israel). Perhaps Matthew wished to contrast their crowd with Jesus' crowd of Galileans, whom these same priests feared. Jesus' quiet response to Judas showed how his followers should respond later to similar betrayals (10:17f.). So, too, his rebuke to the man who used the sword was intended to rule out any reliance on violence by later Christians (5:38-48). The subsequent verse (26:53) assumes, as does the temptation story (4:6), that Jesus had adequate power as Son of God to escape his vocation; this assumption made all the more emphatic his steadfast refusal to use this power. Only his full acceptance of suffering and death can explain why he did not resist arrest. His battle with both Satan and God had been fought and won in the preceding prayers. Now, after the arrival of Judas, his only word to Judas was the simple direct question, Why? His only reaction to the crowds was a mild comment on their cowardice and their misunderstanding. His most brusque criticism was aimed at a disciple who had so mistaken his kingdom as to suppose it could be defended by the sword.

Trial and Denial (26:57—27:10)

The narrative of Peter's denial (26:57-75) is woven tightly into the account of the trial, perhaps to contrast sharply how Jesus and his chief disciple responded to the same dilemmas. The account of the trial itself leaves many questions unanswered; an Evangelist had no interest in many of them. Was it legal for the council to meet at night? If not, was this meeting more of an informal gathering to find a charge that could be presented the next morning to the Roman governor? Did these respected leaders really seek a *false* charge so that the whole matter was a frame-up? If no disciples were present, how did they later secure a reliable account of the proceedings? Was there really no ground for the charge that Jesus was an enemy of the temple (21:41-42; 23:35; 24:1-2)? Why did he refuse to answer the false charges? Did he or did he not confess himself to be the Messiah in the enigmatic reply, "You have said so"? And why should his prophecy of the coming of the Son of man have been considered blasphemy? Should this prophecy be trusted when he could not even answer the simple question, when blindfolded, "Who struck you?" Yes, there are many more questions than answers. Yet the story conveys an indelible impression by its grim statement of the basic antithesis: the religious leaders with their power, their self-righteousness, their self-deceptions growing out of a profound challenge to their own interests—all this on one hand; and on the other, a single, silent "false" prophet, without position or prestige, without any visible evidence of God's support. One other point: In reading this story of the trial we should remember that this same prophet had predicted his disciples would soon confront similar crises (10:17-18; 24:9-10). This prediction Matthew knew had come true.

To Matthew, it was Peter who proved to be false; his fall is described with unrelieved candor (26:69-75). A maid's suspicion was sufficient to undo him. Unlike the charge against Jesus, this charge was simply that of association with Jesus: Peter was a Galilean and an accomplice of *the* Galilean. Such a charge implies that the movement had become so strong in this province as to throw suspicion on all who used that dialect. Although Peter was the bravest of the twelve, his fears proved too strong for him (was the story in 14:22-32 an anticipation of this?). His threefold lie fulfilled Jesus' prediction (26:34) and stands in bleak antithesis to the threefold prayer of Jesus in Gethsemane. His words, "I don't know the man," are dramatic counterparts to the words of the Son of man in the final judgment, "I never knew you" (7:23; 25:12). After the exit of Peter there was no further direct contact between Jesus and the twelve until they met on the mountain (28:16). All had happened according to God's will, yet this fact heightened rather than lessened the culpability of those who shared in delivering Jesus to be crucified; and the guilt of the leaders of Israel was less terrible to Matthew than the guilt of Peter and his comrades. Perhaps Peter's tears (26:75) said as much.

The individual stories of only two disciples—Peter and Judas—received mention in the basic narrative of the cross. In their weaknesses both gave unwitting testimonies to the strength of Jesus. Both found themselves fulfilling Jesus' realistic warnings. Both were led by their treachery to a new level of self-awareness, to profound repentance and confession. In neither case does Matthew express vindictive hatred against them for their treachery. The portrait of Judas (27:3-

10) reflects several striking motifs: his spontaneous testimony to the innocence of Jesus, even before Jesus' death (in fact his own death seems to have preceded that of Jesus); the priests' awareness of the uncleanness of the blood money, signifying their implicit recognition of Jesus' innocence; Judas' agreement with Jesus, as confirmed by Judas' suicide, that it would be better had he never been born (26:24; 27:3-10). Because a cemetery was considered an unclean place, contaminating those who visited it, it was appropriate that unclean money be used to buy it. Because Jesus and his followers were aliens within the community it was appropriate that this cemetery be allotted to indigent strangers. Most germane, however, in the Synoptists' minds was the fulfillment of prophecy that came about in this decision on how to spend the defiled money (Zechariah 11:12f.; Jeremiah 32:6-15). Again the events of the Passion fulfilled the scriptures, but these same scriptures did not enable anyone to anticipate the mode of fulfillment.

Crucifixion of a King (27:11-54)

Just as the stories of Peter and Judas were woven into the actions of the Sanhedrin, so now the stories of "the people" were dovetailed into the account of the hearing before Pilate (27:11-26). The Roman governor served as procurator of Judea from A.D. 26 to 36. As the representative of Rome, Pilate was charged with halting any seditious movement within this occupied country. Because he was a gentile, this moment marked the delivering over to the gentiles of one who had come to save Israel (20:19; 24:9). It was Jesus' form of giving his testimony, albeit silently, to non-Jewish rulers. In this testimony the twelve would one day join (10:18; 24:14; 28:19). Jesus refused to defend himself in this situation but left the outcome wholly to his judge. The baffling "You have said so [27:11]" should probably be taken as a noncommittal answer, which forced Pilate to make his own decision.

The narrative includes Pilate among those who in one way or another recognized the innocence of Jesus. The innocence is repeatedly implied in the story—in the comment of 27:18, in the request of Pilate's wife, in the skeptical question of verse 23, and finally in the gesture of washing his hands (which, like many other phrases in this story, has entered our common stock of idiomatic expressions). Pilate's guilt stems from his willingness to crucify an innocent man, his fear of the priests and the mob, his abdication of responsibility for the administration of justice by releasing a notorious criminal in exchange for an innocent victim. His act of freeing Barabbas was, of course, an act of consummate weakness and of gross injustice.

The account of the release of Barabbas imputes similar traits to the priests and to the crowds, who were their dupes. It had already become clear that Jesus was innocent of their charges and that they had been guilty of envy (27:18), because, as Christians told the story, what had been at stake throughout was their status as divinely authorized leaders of God's people (21:33-43). Now it becomes apparent that they had turned the crowds into puppets who did their bidding without question. These crowds were deaf to allegations of Jesus' innocence (v. 23) and were eager to accept the guilt for killing an innocent man. "His blood" did not rest on his own head, in just punishment for his deeds; it would rest on theirs and their children's, in fulfillment of his prophecy, in 23:27-36.

Because the dreadful acceptance of guilt for this judicial murder has contributed so much venom to Christian-Jewish relations through the centuries, several comments are needed here. What were the original intentions of Matthew, writing as he did in a period when his churches were tiny cells struggling for survival in a hostile world?

1. He was primarily concerned to show that the innocence of Jesus was agreed on by all the actors in the story.

2. He was also convinced of the sins of *all* these actors, including gentiles as well as Jews, disciples as well as nondisciples.

3. The self-incrimination of 27:25, attributed to "the people" (*laos*), did not, in this context, apply to the whole religious

community of Israel, but to the crowds (*ochloi*), who on this occasion had been collected by the Sanhedrin to support their conspiracy.

4. Neither Jesus nor Matthew used the guilt of men (whether Judas or Caiaphas, Pilate or Peter, the men who had fled or those who had now gathered for the kill) as grounds for resentment, bitterness, hatred, or violent resistance. The sins of Jesus' adversaries were covered by his compassion both in word (23:37-39) and in deed (26:28). There is no evidence that Jesus violated his own commands to love enemies (5:38-48) or that Matthew repudiated these commands in his effort to provide Christian scribes with the tragic story of Jesus' death.

5. The question of guilt for his death is, after all, decisive only for those who recognize his innocence and his authority as God's son. For such persons the issue immediately becomes one that must be applied to their own case: Are *we* guilty or not? Repentant or not? Forgiven or not?

The attendants of Pilate, like those of the Sanhedrin (26:67-68), greeted the judicial verdict with an explosion of violence and ridicule (27:27-31). Even the account of this brutal mockery was preserved by Christian narrators as conveying in its ironic way a tribute to Jesus' innocence and dignity. The cruel jibes disclosed simultaneously a great lie and a great truth. He *was* a true prophet, although he refused to prophesy on demand (26:67-68). He *was* a king, even though his coronation was celebrated by his enemies. Was his royal robe scarlet, or washed white in his own blood? Did he have a crown, and if so, of what was the crown made? Did he wield the scepter of royal power, and if so, who gave it to him? What form of adoration and genuflexion was appropriate in the presence of such a monarch? One must conclude that the soldiers would not have treated him thus if they had thought him a genuine heir to kingship; therefore, he was innocent of the charge on which he was executed. Yet he was in fact the king of the Jews and worthy of all these tokens of kingship; therefore, they were guilty of the grossest forms of cruelty. Yet Jesus accepted this grotesque charade and used it to give an authentic testimony to the gentiles. The narrative could welcome the irony, because it showed how this "criminal" immediately converted all these brutal insults into messianic glory.

Irony remains the dominant mood in the account of the procession to Golgotha and the brutal dialogues there (27:32-44). It becomes more evident when one recalls the other Simon (last seen in 26:75), the rule regarding discipleship (16:24), and the notice that this Simon was *compelled* to carry the cross. So, too, there are hidden nuances in the comments on Jesus' thirst, his clothing, the words affixed to the cross, and the companionship with the two robbers, who in their extremity joined in the taunts. This irony comes to a climax in the careful wording of the taunts. Although the ribald vituperation disclosed blindness to the truth, it served to verify the truth. For example, the crucifixion becomes the occasion on which the temple is being destroyed and rebuilt (cp. John 2:19; Matthew 27:51; Acts 17:24; 1 Corinthians 3:16). Because Jesus was the Son of God he did not save himself by coming down from the cross (4:1-11). Only because he was unable to save himself could he save others. Faith in him would be produced not by the display of his power, but by unmistakable evidence of this total self-sacrifice. His trust in God was fully vindicated and not betrayed, although this vindication would require a revelation from God (11:25-30) before human beings would see it.

From the sixth to the ninth hour is, when measured from sunrise, from noon to midafternoon. Darkness came when the sun should have been brightest, a symbol of the apocalyptic reversal of things (27:45-54). Did this death mark the darkest hour in human history, or did it mark the end of night? Or did the dark and the light meet here? Regardless of precise nuances, these verses need to be related to the general theme of night and day in the early Christian lexicon (e.g., Matthew 4:16; 5:14; 6:23; 10:27; Luke 2:32; John 1:4-9; 3:19f.; 12:35-46; 1 Peter 2:9). Here the darkness is linked to the cry of dereliction and to the moments leading to death. The story brings into play the cosmic as well as the human signs of cataclysm. Some of these had been traditionally accepted as authentic signs of the dawning of the new age. For example, the darkening of the sun had been mentioned as recently as 24:29. So, too, the earthquake (24:7; 28:2; Revelation 6:12; 8:5; 11:13). Only Matthew records the opening of the tombs, the raising of the saints, and the entrance into the holy city. These, too, were frequent features of prophetic visions of the messianic age (Revelation 3:10-12; 7:14-17; 11:4-13; 21:2-14). It may be questioned whether this type of event was readily visible to bystanders. Only profound meditation could penetrate the mystery of what happened and grasp the hidden repercussions of Jesus' death. Apart from God's help, bystanders did not see anything extraordinary in this event. Otherwise these verses (51-53) would seem to contradict the truth implicit in verses 40 to 50, that no visible proofs would be offered to demonstrate the divine status of Jesus. Because Matthew viewed the trial and execution as the prophesied form of Jesus' testimony to the gentiles (10:18; 24:14), he probably understood the confession of the centurion and his band as evidence that this testimony had begun immediately to produce conversions, starting in the least likely places—with the commander of the squad that executed this "enemy of the people."

Final Mandate (27:55—28:20)

It is fitting that this first gentile "convert" after Jesus' death should have been gained without the help of the disciples. It is also significant that attention shifts back to followers only after Jesus' death, and then to the women rather than to the men. Among the Galileans who had accompanied Jesus to Jerusalem were many women, of whom three are named. Curiously, the mother of Jesus is not included (as in John 19:25f.), and Matthew had not mentioned either of the two Marys earlier but only the third woman, the mother of two disciples (cp. 20:20), who did not share in the later action (27:61; 28:2). Part of Matthew's ironic treatment of the twelve was that it was not they, but the women, who had the courage and the faith to stand by at the crucifixion, albeit at a distance. Moreover, their presence seems to have been occasioned by their duties as deacons (27:55), duties that included the traditional care of the corpse (Luke 23:56). They were, however, soon to be needed for a more momentous task (28:10).

Only in the Passion story does this Joseph appear (Mark 15:43; Luke 23:50; John 19:38). He was a rich man; presumably, only a wealthy man would own a rock tomb. He came from Arimathea, being the first non-Galilean mentioned by Matthew as having followed Jesus. He had in fact been discipled by Jesus himself (an unusual verb used only here and in 13:52; 28:19). Perhaps we are not far wrong in suggesting that, to Matthew, he was, like the centurion, a man won over by the testimony enacted by Jesus in the trial and crucifixion. However that may be, he immediately took over the dangerous duty which by right should have been done by the twelve who fled.

Only Matthew tells us about the posting of the guard at the tomb (27:62-66) and about their final report (28:11-15). It is likely this story developed among Christians as a rebuttal to a rumor circulating among the synagogues that Jesus' body had been stolen and not raised (28:15). "To this day" indicates the concern in Matthew's day to deal with this current report, which had spread "among the Jews," in order to give an alternate explanation of the Christian testimony to the resurrection. This explanation accused the disciples of stealing the body to be able later to advance the claim that Jesus had risen from the grave. By telling of the presence of a guard at the grave, Christians could discredit the slander. This story thus reflects at least three successive stages in the development of tradition: the Christian proclamation, its refutation by hostile Pharisees, and the Christian rebuttal.

Certain traits of the earlier stories appear here. It is the priests and Pharisees who take the initiative. They assumed Jesus could be proved an impostor if his prophecy of resurrection could be disproved. (The reference of 27:63 is to 12:40; 16:21; 17:23; 20:19.) They also assumed his resurrection was impossible and that if they could demonstrate another explanation of an empty tomb they would be able to discredit the disciples' message. However, the same irony continues here, notably in the idea that by their clever devices religious leaders could defeat the purpose of God. The whole idea of security, "order the sepulchre to be made secure," disclosed their own insecurity.

The story of Sunday's events is the continuation and climax of all that had preceded. These events took place at dawn, symbolic, for Matthew, of the new age (28:1-16). The way had been prepared for the two women to see the earthquake and to hear the message from the angel. Both are traditionally ways of indicating the intervention of transcendent heavenly powers into earthly affairs (cp. the transfiguration, 17:1-9), eliciting from human participants typical reactions of fear, trembling, awe, stupor, bewilderment. The focus of attention here may be found in the message of the angel to the women, and especially that part of the message which Jesus himself repeated. No effort is made to describe what happened at the moment of resurrection. The rolling back of the stone door of the tomb was not so much to permit the body to emerge as to enable the women to see that Jesus was no longer inside. The angel took pains to note that the resurrection had happened in vindication of Jesus' own prophecy and in defeat of the Pharisaic plot (27:63f.). Yet the interest of the reader is directed not so much to the victory over death as to the initiation of new plans. It is in this connection that the women received a special assignment—conveying important instructions to the disciples, who must follow him to Galilee and be ready for a rendezvous there.

There seems a conscious design in shaping this conclusion of the document. From the grave two reports had been carried back to the major antagonists by those who had been guarding the tomb: the soldiers and the women. The soldiers gave their testimony to the priests and elders (28:11-13). Their plans had miscarried, their opposition had proved futile, so their only response was further lying, bribery, and conspiracy. The account of their action stresses the innocence of their adversaries and their own guilt.

The women's actions provided a strong contrast; their fear was linked to great joy, reverence, humility, and worship. They ran to complete their task without any thought of concealment or deception. Their message reached its target and produced obedience on the part of the disciples. In Matthew's day the successors of the twelve and the leaders of Israel remained locked in controversy over the issue of the actuality of Jesus' resurrection, his authority, and his mandate. Thus the pictures of these two groups on Easter Sunday continued to characterize the period during which the mandate remained in force.

In the closing paragraph the Gospel reaches a fitting literary end (28:16-20). If this paragraph were deleted, the earlier narrative would become incomplete; with this paragraph the reader is enabled to see the goal toward which all the earlier chapters have been looking. It marks the end not only of the story of Jesus, but of the training of the twelve as well. Interest now shifts from his ministry to theirs (cf. Supplement 5). This mandate placed them in a position comparable to that faced by their Master after his temptation and after the death of the Baptist. Now the manual for missionaries (chap. 10) became effective (except for the limitation of their journey to Israel). From him they have now learned how people can be discipled. The five earlier sermons provided them with the agenda of commands to be taught and obeyed. This mandate set them *above* those who would be baptized by them, but it set them *under* him in whose name they would exercise authority. The mandate was prefaced by a statement regarding Jesus' authority. One may well ask how this statement should be understood, as compared with the earlier exercise of his authority. Did the resurrection mean that now Jesus' authority had become unlimited, covering all contingencies? Or did it mean that God now conferred an authority in heaven to supplement Jesus' earlier authority on earth (cp. 7:29; 9:6, 8)? Did full authority in both heaven and earth enable Jesus to be present with his emissaries always and whenever they obeyed his command? Whatever the answer, this mandate indicates that the decisive impact of the resurrection was to be seen in the final authorization of the mission to all nations, in the ultimate accent on baptism and obedience to his commands, and in his continuing nearness to those whom he had made "prophets, wise men, and scribes" within the churches. Matthew had by no means forgotten the behavior of the twelve during the preceding days; yet on this occasion Jesus makes no mention of it. Such a silence leads us to suppose that Jesus' triumph over his enemies, as well as over the disciples' treachery, would now be adequate evidence of the power of his church to prevail over the gates of Hades (16:16f.), even though the recipients of the keys should prove as derelict as their predecessors (23:15f.). The last word of Matthew celebrates this triumph and therefore this confidence.

Appendix A

NOTES FOR TEACHERS

Chapter I: Introduction to the Gospel

Chapter I is designed for you more than for your class. The chief objective is to acquaint you with the content and organization of the Gospel. In this connection it is highly important for you first to read the Gospel itself several times and then to test my outline of books One to Five by your own observations. This is the best preparation for the first discussion with the class.

For the class, as a background for this discussion, the following steps are important:

1. Read the entire Gospel at a single sitting in an unfamiliar translation (either *Revised Standard Version, New American Bible, New English Bible, Jerusalem Bible,* or *New International Version*). At least two hours are required for this uninterrupted reading.
2. While this reading is fresh in your mind jot down your most important reactions to the Gospel *as a whole.* What made it difficult to read, or easy, or confusing, or interesting, or surprising?
3. Reread the Gospel, looking for major transition points where important shifts appear in time, place, personnel, ideas, literary form, etc. An example is the break between 2:23 and 3:1.
4. Make a list of from ten to fifteen of these transitions and bring the list to class, so students may see the degree of consensus in locating these points.

In the discussion (which may take more than one session) the teacher can choose either to invite students to share their reactions to the Gospel as a whole (#2 above) or to discover the extent of agreement as to major breaks in the narrative line (#4) as a means of testing my outline (pp. 22-23).

With some classes it may prove of interest to the students to test how well they now remember the contents of the Gospel; in this case, the teacher may use the following test. After the class has filled in the blanks it may be worth discussing common errors (e.g., how we are inclined in reading one Gospel to include within it some story that is found only in another Gospel).

SAMPLE TEST

1. Complete the following texts as they appear in Matthew:
   Jesus was born in_____in the days of_____the king.
   His name shall be called_____. (two answers are correct)
   Rise, take the child and flee to_____.
   Woe to you_____, hypocrites.
   _____came by night and stole him away while we were asleep.
   Pilate said, "Whom do you want me to release for you,_____?"
   I will strike the shepherd and_____.

2. Who said the following:
   _____Out of Egypt have I called my son.
   _____Man shall not live by bread alone.
   _____Lord, if you will, you can make me clean.
   _____He casts out demons by the prince of demons.
   _____You brood of vipers...(two answers are correct)
   _____Give me the head of John the Baptist.
   _____If you wish, I will make three booths here.
   _____There are eunuchs who have made themselves eunuchs for the sake of the kingdom of heaven.
   _____I will go before you to Galilee.
   _____Hail, King of the Jews.

3. Number the following texts in the order in which they appear in Matthew (*if* they appear there):

___The transfiguration

___The Last Supper

___A trip to Egypt

___The feeding of the
five thousand

___An appointment of
apostles

___A conversation with a
Samaritan woman

___The parable of the final
judgment

___The Sermon on the Mount

___The parable of the
prodigal son

___The cleansing of the
temple

___A promise of the keys to
Peter

___Satan's offer to Jesus of
the kingdoms of the world

Chapter II: Traditions Concerning the Origin of Jesus

It is important for the students, before coming together for discussion of Matthew 1—2, to prepare for the discussion. They should be urged to:

1. reread the two chapters carefully.
2. remove from their memories, so far as possible, the Lucan narratives of the infancy of Jesus.
3. read in the Old Testament context the predictions referred to by Matthew.
4. locate in Matthew answers to these questions:
    a. Which aspects in these stories are most difficult for you to accept?
    b. Would Matthew's first readers have found them equally difficult to accept. Why or why not?
    c. Why do you think Matthew included these stories in his Gospel?

If a member of the class volunteers for an extra assignment, you might ask him or her to report on the most extensive recent study of these chapters in Raymond E. Brown, *The Birth of the Messiah* (New York: Doubleday, 1977).

For the class session, you may invite members to share the answers they have given to the three questions stated above. Or you may get their reactions to my answers to the two questions on p. 35. In either case, aim at encouraging a

145

vigorous and uninhibited discussion of the problems the students have encountered. It is too early to seek verbal agreement on the multiple historical and doctrinal problems the birth stories themselves pose.

Finally, ask the class whether the birth stories in Matthew illustrate the truth of one of the following statements:

- "Grace shatters the calculations of legalism and comes to us as a surprise [F. Craddock, *Overhearing the Gospel* (Nashville: Abingdon Press, 1978), p. 87]."
- "The God who is coming is altogether different from the one that man expects. He is not the God whom memory, reason or imagination anticipates.... Religiously initiated and educated man is completely deceived.... The unexpected comes at the core of the expected. The presence is elusive but real [Samuel Terrien, *The Elusive Presence* (New York: Harper & Row, 1978), p. 234]."
- "In fact God's revelation destroys every picture which man's desires make of it, so that the real test of man's desire for salvation is to believe even when God encounters him in a totally different way from that he expected [Rudolf Bultmann, *The Gospel of John* (Philadelphia: Westminster Press, 1971), p. 228]."

If the connections between the stories and these quotations are too obscure, the materials in Supplement 1 may help to clarify those connections.

Chapter III: Beginnings in the Work of Salvation

So much is covered in these five chapters that you may choose to allow your students to discuss whatever reactions they may have had; or you may wish to focus attention on a specific saying or two in the Manual for Church Members by asking the group which of the sayings provides the best summary of the manual, such as one of the following: 5:20; 5:48; 6:10; 6:24; 7:12; 7:24. Three other types of study may be suggested:

1. Most of the separate teachings in these chapters were designed in such a way as to aid in their memorization; their

present form also reflects an extensive reliance on memory among early Christians. As a result, students are usually surprised at the ease with which they can still be memorized, even in an age that relies on reading and writing. A class may demonstrate this fact by repeating one of the following sayings three times consulting the text, and then three times without looking: 7:7; 7:12; 6:24; 6:14-15; 5:43-44.

2. In discussing the earlier chapters we noted the presence of "the broken chain." Events take place in fulfillment of the scripture, yet such events could not be anticipated as representing such fulfillment. To help each student test the presence of the same feature in chapters 5 to 7 set up this experiment:

a. Ask them to put on the top line of four separate sheets of paper the four separate statements in 5:17-20.

b. Ask them to classify each teaching under *one* of these four statements: e.g., 7:12 seems to belong under 5:17; 6:2 belongs under 5:20.

c. When all or most of the separate teachings have been so classified, let each student formulate his or her answer to the following questions: How and why did these teachings fulfill the law and the prophets (5:17)? How and why did the scribes and Pharisees, whose special training lay in the interpretation of scripture, fail to recognize this fulfillment, but instead charged Jesus (and Matthew's Christians) with the abolition of the law?

3. Whenever a group gives detailed attention to all the teachings in this manual a typical reaction is this: "How impossible! No human community can reasonably be expected to obey these uncompromising demands." First, then, allow the class to express this reaction and to specify the commands that seem impossible. A second typical reaction to this manual, and to Jesus' message as a whole, centers in the announcement that God's kingdom is at hand (4:17), and that it is immediately accessible to "the poor in spirit" (5:3), and in fact that all

things will be given to those who seek first this kingdom. "How can the kingdom of God appear in a world where there has been no tangible change in human affairs—when injustice and cruelty, when starvation and warfare, are as powerful as ever?" Allow the class to express this reaction and to say how God's kingdom seems as remote as ever. Now, as a third step, ask whether there is any connection between these two "impossibilities." Does God's kingdom seem so impossible because God's people consider the beatitudes impossible goals? Or does God's kingdom first become accessible when the people choose to enter the narrow gate (7:13) by obeying these commands? What is the relation between the fulfillment of God's will in history and the people's obedience to God's will as disclosed in Jesus? In this discussion the Lord's Prayer (6:9-12) may provide one answer.

Chapter IV: The Physician and the Crowds

These materials are so provocative that you may need nothing to elicit discussion, but you may need to guide the discussion so it consists of something beyond the sharing of familiar notions that students have brought to their reading of the text (e.g., Did these miracles happen exactly as recorded?). I suggest two possible areas for exploration.

1. Locate in chapters 8 and 9 some of the key symbols, and appraise the value of these symbols to Matthew in his work of teaching. Among the many symbols some of the following may have meanings the students have not stopped to consider: blindness, wineskins, wedding feast, leprosy, paralysis, storm, boat, sparrows, burying one's father, dumbness, harvest, hemorrhage, flute players, taxes. Having developed the recognition of symbolic language, you may wish to ask the class if there are any connections between these symbols and the teachings in chapters 5 to 7.

2. In the text I have suggested that in chapter 10 a reader may discern many different situations the twelve would face in fulfilling their assignments. The class may test this obser-

vation by listing as many situations as they can spot (.e.g., flogging in the synagogues, v. 17). Then they may ask how many of these situations were current in Matthew's day.

Sooner or later the class will want to discuss Matthew's idea of the second coming of Jesus and the final judgment. Whenever the time seems best to discuss this topic, you will find help in Supplement 3.

Chapter V: The Mysterious Presence of the Kingdom

1. If you make advance assignments to the class, I suggest you ask them to collect and classify all the terms in 11:2—13:52 that Matthew used to describe those who responded positively to Jesus. You may then check their lists with the following list, which is complete and in sequence: the blind, the lame, lepers, the deaf, the dead, the poor, babes, those who labor, the heavy-laden, a man with a withered hand, the gentiles, blind and dumb demoniac, good men, those doing the will of God, the seed falling on good soil, the righteous, the sons of the kingdom, a man buying a field or a pearl, edible fish. The class may wish to discuss the variety of images and their common focus. Recalling the analogy of the split TV screen (above, p.12), is it possible to think of Matthew's church as composed of these same types of members? Are readers to infer that the living Lord is present with his church *only* if this church continues to include these types.

2. Or you may focus attention on the work of the scribe-healers. In chapter 10 they are assigned to a healing ministry; in chapter 13, to a scribal role (esp. 13:10-17) of teachers who can see and hear what is hidden from others. Are we to infer that these two roles support each other? If this knowledge of kingdom secrets (13:11) qualified them to heal the sick (10:8), how are we to understand these healings? If their work of healing qualified them to penetrate the mysteries of the kingdom, what light does this throw on the mysteries? Is there a similar connection between a modern minister's work of healing and teaching? How does ability to see enable one to heal (13:15)?

Chapter VI: The Care of the Crowds

You may ask students to prepare for class discussion in one of two ways:

1. In examining 13:53—19:1 they could make a list of all the disciples' weaknesses, all the temptations they faced, whether implicit or explicit. Students should keep these filed according to text, so that in class a full list may be compiled. There are at least five in chapter 14, four in chapter 15, four in chapter 16, two in chapter 17, and eight in chapter 18. In class discussion you may discuss what it was in the situation that made these temptations inevitable, or culpable, or essential to their training as Jesus' representatives?

2. Selecting one single episode (17:1-8) they could make a list of the links connecting this event to earlier or later events—to the birth stories, to the scriptures (Moses and Elijah, the law and the prophets), to what happened on other mountains, to other revelations from heaven, to the disciples, to the resurrection. An objective in class discussion is to make clear how many potential overtones a story like this has.

Chapter VII: Preparation for the Passion

1. The parables in these chapters are fascinating. The students will be prompted to analyze the detail of these parables, if you ask them to select (a) the parable that reflects the clearest picture of the Matthean church, (b) the parable that reflects the clearest picture of this church's rivals, and (c) to list the reasons for the selection.

2. These chapters, especially chapter 23, provide an opportunity to discuss the basis for anti-Semitism within the Christian church. For many readers, this Gospel is intensely anti-Semitic; undoubtedly, it has enabled many modern Christians to claim scriptural support for their hostility to Jews. The class may be asked to locate in these chapters the evidence—pro and con—then perhaps to discuss the question of the degree to which modern Jews are linked to the first-century Pharisees and our own churches are linked to the Matthean church.

Chapter VIII: Covenant and Mandate

The Passion story is a story so filled with meanings, whether tragic or glorious, that words of interpretation are, at best, pathetic efforts to capture ineffable truth. Class discussion of so majestic a drama can quickly degenerate into banal and trivial gossip. One way to prevent such degeneration is to turn to nonverbal forms of expression. Three of such forms are readily accessible.

1. *Hymn book.* Ask each member of the class to suggest three hymns that seem best to catch the mood and spirit of the Matthean Last Supper.

2. *Visual art.* Ask each member to nominate one or two paintings of the crucifixion that follow satisfactorily the account in Matthew.

3. *Music.* Arrange a session when the class can listen to a good recording of J.S. Bach's *The Passion According to St. Matthew.* They should listen with a copy of the Matthew text in their hands. Afterward they can share their reactions with regard to Bach's interpretation (cf. Supplement 6).

Appendix B

SUPPLEMENTS

Supplement 1: On Interpreting the Birth Stories

(The following excerpt is from an essay that appeared in *Theology Today* 7 [1950], pp. 358-75.)

Among the more problematic sections of the New Testament are the nativity stories in Matthew and Luke. Neither contemporary historians nor their audiences know quite what to do with these accounts. Most historians and most readers raise questions which the stories do not answer, while the questions which are answered are not those in which most readers are interested. On hearing or reading the accounts of Jesus' birth, they will usually ask: "What actually happened? Did these things occur in exactly the way described?" Satisfactory answers to these questions are clearly dependent upon other queries: "Who wrote the accounts? What sort of evidence did he have? Is he a reliable witness?"

As one reads the narratives, one's attention will naturally be drawn to those items that have a bearing upon these questions. Many details will escape notice, but not those which are relevant to the problems in the forefront of one's mind. These problems provide the magnetic poles around which the materials will gravitate. For example, the American reader will not quickly pass over the mention of Mary's virginity, the vision of angels, the guidance by the star. The items thus selected as most problematic serve as an index to the collective unconscious, to the web of assumptions prevalent in a given milieu. Whatever answers may be given, whether credulous or incredulous, the major meaning of the stories will be located within the areas where the major problems have been encountered.

Historians are, of course, apt to pride themselves upon being independent of their public, but such independence is often more superficial than genuine. Whatever the audience, this is one test of their competence as historians: Have they provided adequate answers to the questions raised by that audience? Because the problem is set in terms of the "apperceptive mass" of their audience, neither the historians nor their audience will be really free to listen de novo to the stories themselves, uncolored by prior assumptions.

It is, of course, the function and obligation of interpreters to enlarge the area of their freedom from these attitudes. They should notice things which the casual reader has missed, should raise new questions that break through the fetters of environmental influence, should ignore immediate needs in their concentration upon what may seem to be irrelevant. They can reduce the number of biases that affect their own evaluations, in giving their audience what it really needs rather than what it assumes it wants.

By fulfilling this function for themselves as historians, they also serve to increase the freedom of their readers. The truly critical aspect of their work is expressed not so much through their criticism of primary sources as through their criticism of current conceptions of what happened, whether their own or those of their readers. All critical historians are primarily servants of some contemporary community; apart from their work the true liberty of that community is jeopardized (a liberty from its own hidden dogmatisms).

An unusual opportunity in this respect is open to the interpreters of the birth narratives. Knowledge of the content of these stories is as widely diffused as that of any portion of scripture. Attitudes toward the meaning of the stories are deeply engrained in the public mind. Yet the imagery and the mood of the stories are so alien to our cultural atmospheres that misinterpretations of the original narratives may be found on every hand, each misconception an index to the pattern of unconscious assumptions held by some segment of society. Throughout the wide range of attitudes (complete incredulity, a selective aesthetic appreciation, a tacit agnosticism, an uncertain orthodoxy, complete and aggressive credulity), each reader takes it for granted that *his* or *her* attitude is grounded in the objective content of the stories themselves, whereas it is really dependent upon the particular context into which his or her mind places the story. The Word of God remains free in its power to challenge and to judge the whole orbit of our self-centered reflections, but as we listen to that Word in the birth stories we are seldom free to hear it as a fresh communication of judgment and freedom. Critical historians—however skeptical or conventional—are not wholly free to expound the stories adequately; yet neither may they easily dismiss their obligation to enlarge the area of their freedom by seeking to expound them more adequately.

How shall they do this as historians except by relying upon the tools which their science has sharpened for their use? To be sure, these tools may be faulty, since they too represent a pervasive philosophy of history endemic in some segment of their own culture. Each historical methodology is the product of some particular outlook on history. Nevertheless, the only way for individual historians to protect themselves from their own self-centeredness and that of their confessional group is by rigorous application of this imperfect methodology. In the process of their study, if they remain true critics, they should discover new meanings which they had not suspected, new data which correct the defects in their tools, new perspectives that affect the context of presuppositions with which they began that study. Such discoveries are the mark of genuine liberty. This process may be illustrated in the current studies of the birth narratives. We shall approach these stories first of all as historical critics, and then we shall ask what may happen to these critics and their methods as they pursue their work.

I. THE HISTORIANS' ANALYSIS OF THE STORIES

Let us suppose that these critics begin their work with this objective in mind: to reconstruct what the original writers intended to convey to their initial audience and to recapture how that audience understood this message. Once their aim has been stated in these terms, the historians encounter many obstacles, of which we may indicate three.

1. In dealing with the birth narratives it is particularly difficult to locate the original author. These narratives are the distillation of a community's experience, an articulation of the multiple memories and hopes of that community. They were written down, to be sure, by individual editors, each of whom would shape the tradition in his own way, but this shaping process is so subtle and gradual that we can never be sure exactly what nuances a given author may have added.

2. Even if we could name a particular editor, the matter of his intention may elude us. Seldom does a writer of such stories have a single, conscious, definable purpose. Especially is this true in the work of a church leader, for he fills a very complex role within the household of faith. He stands between his people and God, speaking to God for his people and speaking to his people for God. He is the channel of a tradition that speaks to his own life at countless points before it can speak to his audience. We may detect many motifs in his literary endeavor, but we cannot reduce all these motifs to a single, controlling motive. He has heard God speak through the total impact of the total story. He in turn must tell the whole story so that others may hear the same voice. For him the meanings of the story are inseparable from the story.

3. The objective of recapturing the initial response of the intended audience is subject to similar obstacles. We do not know which community first heard the stories. In fact, they probably circulated in many places and in many forms before they were written down in one place and in one form. What are the historians to do? They may well study the history of the entire Christian community to understand the tensions and pressures under which it lived, its relationship to the Messiah, the Holy Spirit, the world. They may well examine what connotations each of the images and words carried in other contexts. The studies of other folk-literature have produced some helpful techniques, which they may apply in their

attempted reconstruction of the early meanings of the tradition. Let us mention three questions which should be asked.

What was the original *Sitz im Leben* (life situation) for the stories? The raising of this question enables us to eliminate many possibilities. The situation presupposed by the birth stories is not that of an apostle, preaching the Gospel for the first time to unconverted Jews or gentiles; they were used by believers for believers. Nor is the primary context provided by the work of an apologete, defending Christian convictions from the attacks of pagan adversaries. The stories presuppose faith; they do not argue for certain dogmas but serve as testimonies of those who have been moved to glorify God for the gift of God's Son. It is equally obvious that the narratives do not represent the official work of teachers whose function it was to train new initiates in their new duties. The ethical dilemmas of individual disciples, as well as the usual forms and motifs of the catechism, are lacking. Nor may we easily picture an exorcist using this material as a means for ministering to the sick and demon-possessed. Even more foreign is the suggestion that we should envisage a community archivist, composing carefully documented annals, weaving together the reminiscences of the church into a single strand of successive events.

The exploration of the life situation also eliminates the thought that the stories were directed first of all to children, as winsome ways of appealing to their naïve fancies; the tradition was produced by adults and for adults. Nor was adult use limited to an annual festival of Advent as a periodic means by which parents might escape from the harsh realities of life to the romantic fantasies of infancy. No, this tradition reflects the mature and realistic understanding of the Christian life, based upon the cumulative, year-round experience of the Christian community as a whole. What, then, may we say more positively about the context within which the meanings of the tradition were set by the first hearers?

In the first place, the audience already knows the course of later events in the story of Jesus. The listeners are well acquainted with the preaching of John the Baptist and with the consequences of his ministry. They also well knew the character and sequence of the major episodes in Jesus' ministry. Narrators and listeners alike are thinking backward from the period after the cross, after the resurrection. Nor is it necessarily a flaw in the story that the content of the prophecies was shaped by later experience.

In the second place, the context for the tradition was provided by all the memories of the history of the church, up to the time of each successive reading. The congregation vividly recollects its encounters with Herod and his successors. It has seen in its own life the fulfillment of prophecies, the prevenient grace of God in God's call of the humble. Some members testify that they, too, have been called from their mothers' wombs, that in them God has chosen "even things that are not, to bring to nothing things that are [1 Cor. 1:28]." These members of Christ's body know how God's power appears in the weakest vessels, how that power works through signs and wonders, how the Holy Spirit continues to humble the proud and to exalt the meek. It senses the hidden continuities that link together the coming of Jesus in Bethlehem and the repeated comings at times and places where he is not expected.

In the third place, the apperceptive mass of each individual disciple provides a part of the context in which he interprets the meanings of the tradition. At each new reading, each disciple hears the story as a Word addressed to himself or herself, even though that reading takes place in a corporate assembly. He or she places the story within the frame of personal history, orienting it around recollections of earlier encounters with God's mercy. Even today, as disciples hear the story afresh, they are subject to the struggle between doubt and trust, for they are waging still the battle against principalities and powers. The shape of this present struggle affects the shape of the message they hear, for they are listening with ears which God is training through the discipline of everyday experience. The *Sitz im Leben* thus includes the total content of three stories, fused together: the story of Jesus, of the new Israel, of the believer. To understand the original context, therefore, exegetes must themselves stand at the point of convergence of these three stories. When they take this as their point of standing, they discover that the *Sitz im Leben* has become the *Sitz im Glauben* (faith situation), because to the original narrator and his audience each life situation derives its meaning from its bearing on faith.

To the believing congregation each situation was a faith situation because its significance stemmed from the contemporaneous relationship of that congregation to God, a relationship that was controlled by the memory of Christ's work. The Father of Jesus was even now carrying out through Christ his program for the salvation of the world. Although the plan of this mystery had first been disclosed in the death and exaltation of Jesus, the same invincible purpose had been at work secretly in all the preceding episodes. Since the heart of the mystery was the self-humiliation of God's Son, the initial act of descent carries within itself the whole plan of redemption, and should be understood as such (Philippians 2:5-11). Since each episode of humiliation conceals the whole eternal purpose, the eyes of faith discern in each episode the major accents of that purpose: God's merciful invitation and stern judgment, the offense created by God's Word, the creation of a new Adam and a new Israel, the powers of the new age at work in those who seek that new age with all their heart, the manifestation of glory to the humble. It is thus that the whole Gospel furnished the central motifs in the tradition concerning Jesus' birth. Let us isolate four of these motifs:

First of all, we may note that the stories articulate the conviction that in the coming of Jesus God moves decisively toward people in a loving intent to save them. Over all the various incidents stands the sign "God with us [Matt. 1:23]." All the happenings participate in the same miracle; all are transfigured by the light of a single mystery. To the external gaze of human beings, nothing appears to have changed in the balance of human fortunes, but God's visit nevertheless produces a total change in the significance of all history. The story of the Son's descent to earth becomes for faith an epitome of how all history is incorporated into a single grand design.

A second major motif of the stories, when placed in the context of the *Sitz im Glauben,* is to express the varying responses of creation to this divine activity. In the wary cruelty of Herod may be seen the fear of God's kingdom and the blind efforts to protect one's own autonomy (Matthew 2:13-18). In Joseph one is led to appreciate the temptation to be offended by the breach in prevailing moral standards and the overcoming of that temptation by trust in the heavenly command (Matthew 1:20-24). In the readiness of the shepherds to follow the angel's directions, the believers saw a paradigm of the way in which they should await the promised sign of redemption (Luke 2:15-20). The symphonic score has a place for all sorts of contrapuntal variations, for the dissonances of unbelief, but penetrating all these may be heard the dominant chords. Each movement is the occasion for people to magnify and glorify God (Matthew 2:2, 11; Luke 1:46; 2:13, 20, 28), for them to stand in fear and trembling before God (Luke 1:12, 29, 64; 2:9), to give thanks for God's mercy (Luke 1:64, 68; 2:38), to rejoice greatly (Luke 1:14, 44, 46, 58; 2:10; Matthew 2:10), and to receive God's peace (Luke 1:79; 2:14).

A third dominant motif in the *Sitz im Glauben* is the clear recollection of Jesus' place in the whole history of salvation. In the babe in his cradle is realized the solidarity of Israel in the one new man; all the generations of faith meet here in a final unity. The stories declare how in Christ God has fulfilled the promises to the fathers: to Adam (Luke 3:38), to Abraham (Matthew 1:1, 17; Luke 1:55, 73), to Jacob (Luke 1:33), to David (Matthew 1:1, 17; Luke 1:32; 2:4, 11). They link the ministry of Jesus to that of prophets and kings (Luke 1:17, 32; 2:4, 11; Matthew 1:23; 2:5, etc.). They relate the new covenant to the sacrifices in the temple (Luke 1:8f.; 2:22, 41f.) and to the fulfillment of the Torah (Luke 1:6; 2:22, 27). They constitute one way of saying with Paul that the Son of God was born of woman, born under the law, born of the flesh. Yet at the same time the narrative expresses the conviction that Jesus was born both of the flesh and of the Spirit, that he was a son of Israel-according-to-the-flesh and of Israel-according-to-the-Spirit, for in him the two became one. In other words, the stories maintain throughout the effective priority of God's Word; election comes through faith in God's grace and not through the flesh, although the flesh is chosen as the medium of that grace. One further link between the birth story and the whole story of salvation is this: The nativity narrative prefigures the later ministry of Jesus. In Luke it anticipates his later mission of healing and forgiveness to the sick, the poor, the captives; in Matthew it anticipates the final conflict with earthly rulers and their final discomfiture. For the congregation the stories proclaimed the cross and the resurrection (Luke 2:33-35).

A fourth aspect of the *Sitz im Glauben* may now be mentioned, albeit too briefly. Those who told and heard the stories of Jesus' nativity were themselves ministers of reconciliation to others. They were sent to proclaim the gospel of God's peace to their fellows, a proclamation by deed as well as by word. They were themselves signs to an evil generation of what God was doing. On one side were the Herods and all the forces of evil; on the other was a babe. In this context the stories sounded a shout of defiance at the enemies of the cross, and a shout of victory over their power. To be sure, they were not used to win over the Herods, but they exerted a strong influence over the martyrs. To them they conveyed an understanding of suffering, a new love for the hostile world, and a new ability to join in the hallelujahs of faith.

The stories thus lead the historians back to their original context, through the life situation to the faith situation to the worship situation where they belong, and where their significance is to be grasped. Now what are the exegetes to do here? How will they fulfill their function of reconstructing the original meaning of this historical data? Let us suppose that they now realize several things. They realize the intricate interdependence between the narratives and the life of this community. They become aware that any interpretation of the stories to be genuinely adequate must evoke a repetition of this situation. They recognize that such a repetition is something which they must share as worshipers before they can describe God's works as interpreters. Finally, they become conscious of the fact that they themselves, as servants of the church, are responsible for the reenactment of that worship situation. When they arrive at this point, they may find that the stories themselves begin to exert an unexpected and curious judgment upon their previous outlook as historians. We will look briefly at some of the forms which this judgment may take and the changes which it may produce.

II. THE STORIES' ANALYSIS OF THE HISTORIANS

One may perhaps trace all the changes in orientation to the transposition of contexts. On beginning their study the exegetes place the object of their study within the context of their own thought-world; they set this event with which they are dealing into the frame of historical process. They relate the data to their previous body of knowledge as a whole. They think of their task as one small segment in their professional assignment. And all this is necessary and justified because the birth of Jesus is an event like all others in its historical conditionedness and particularity. But when in faith and worship they hear God speak afresh through these stories to them, in the midst of their own concerns, an entire frame of meaning is disclosed which establishes itself as a rightful context for their own work. Not only do they see that God's purpose, as revealed in the incarnation, encompasses all history; not only do they realize that Christ is even now extending his sovereignty through the events of space and time; not only do they realize that the Christian community is the pattern according to which God is reconstituting all communities; but they also realize that they themselves and their work as historians belong within this context. In hearing the birth narratives they have heard God's own verdict concerning what is the true context for their own work. How, then, does this affect their perspective as historians?

Let it be said that their profession as historians continues, as does their selection of the best methods for study of ancient literary documents. In fact they are now under greater obligation to be accurate and competent historians, for theirs is the task of preserving, correcting, and enhancing the memories of the church. The more seriously they consider their work as a service of the Lord, so much the more vigorously will they seek freedom from their own self-centered ideas and wishes. Well they know how easily the memories of the church may be corrupted and how, especially in its sentimental use of the birth stories, the Christian congregation cloaks its unwitting heresies under romantic platitudes and dogmatic truisms. In counteracting the current misunderstandings of the narratives, they will find ample use for the sharpest tools.

Certain objectives, however, which they formerly held may now seem to be condemned. To the extent that their motive had been that of enhancing their own professional reputations, or gaining a public for themselves, or establishing their superiority over other scholars, to that extent the stories themselves may call the historians to repentance. To the extent that they have assumed their own elevation above the materials, their own ability to judge, to select, to condemn, to approve; to the extent that they have shared modernism's implicit disdain for the ancient, or sophistication's supercilious attitude toward the primitive, or the rationalist's suspicions of the imaginative truths of sagas and poetry—to that extent the stories will call for a new mind.

There also may take place a revision of the central questions with which they began their study. No longer is it enough to ask, "What happened?" No longer is it enough to try to delete from the record the secondary elements, leaving only such facts as historians may rate as authentic. Rather, considering the wealth of meaning disclosed by the stories, individual historians may ask: "How can I mediate to people of my own generation such an effective understanding of what God has done for the world in Christ? How can I remove the hindrances which prevent the church from hearing in these stories the same message which God spoke to the fathers in faith? How can I grasp afresh the meaning for history of what God has done in history?" Such a transposition of questions may well humble historians, for although this task is more than they can accomplish they will not feel free to go on to less urgent matters until they have accomplished it.

The changed outlook may also affect their choice of methods. Is the former method so oriented that it can only produce results which faith would consider quite trivial or irrelevant? Does the method adequately deal with the quality of inspired imagination that produced the stories? Does it take account of that level of experience where the Holy Spirit is at work? Does it damage the message which the stories tell by forcing it into purely objective categories of what could be photographed and televised, or by reducing it to purely subjective categories of fanciful ideas and fleeting feelings? Only a method that is adjusted to the message will be adequate to it.

Such changes, however, as are produced by a fresh impact of the history should make them better historians. They should now be able to enter more fully into the life of the distant past and to give a better report on the inner structure of that life. They should be able to assess the work of ancient writers more accurately, by viewing that work within the writers' own perspective. They should understand more clearly the writers' function in history, and their own function as successors. This should permit them to see their own work as a work of the whole church, in its effort to keep in order its memories of its past. More significantly, their greater knowledge of the original relevance of the birth narratives should make them more effective critics of current misconceptions of those narratives, misconceptions which are more dangerous to the health of the church than church people are likely to admit. Now, however, when they condemn unsuspected heresies among the devout, they will be speaking in behalf of the original authors.

Perhaps critics will also be freed from the tendency to archaism from which much "orthodoxy" suffers. Though they realize that the original authors told the stories in the best way for them to communicate God's message, and though each repetition of the message requires the context of Christian worship, yet critics as leaders of that worship must do what they can to tell the message in the idiom of their congregations. The prayers and the hymns, if they are to be genuine, must be the deepest and most spontaneous expressions of the congregation's heart. The conversation with God must draw into the story of the incarnation the whole gamut of the congregation's experience. Critics will interpret the message best by showing how modern history belongs within its context. For only when the stories are the medium for a new encounter between God and God's people, only then will they be rightly interpreted.

Supplement 2: On Secret Piety

(The following excerpt is from my book *Commands of Christ* [Nashville: Abingdon Press, 1972], pp. 47-68.)

In the Sermon on the Mount there is a carefully constructed poem of three stanzas dealing with two opposite kinds of religious observance. An arrangement of the three stanzas in three columns (A, B, C) makes the parallel construction clear. The same arrangement illustrates the contrast between one type of piety (lines 1-6) and its opposite (lines 7-11). All three stanzas sharpen the behavior.*

A	B	C
1. When you give alms,	1. When you pray,	1. When you fast,
2. don't be like the hypocrites	2. don't be like the hypocrites;	2. don't be like the hypocrites,
3. for they sound trumpets† before them in the synagogues and in the streets,	3. for they love to stand and pray in the synagogues and at the street corners,	3. for they disfigure their† faces and look dismal

*A more detailed treatment may be found in my book *Commands of Christ* (Nashville: Abingdon Press, 1972), pp. 47-68.
†I have modified the text in these lines to accentuate the parallel constructions, but this has not changed the basic thought.

4. that they may be praised by men.	4. that they may be seen by men.	4. that they may be seen by men.
5. Truly, I say to you,	5. Truly, I say to you,	5. Truly, I say to you,
6. they have their reward.	6. they have their reward.	6. they have their reward.
7. But when you give alms,	7. But when you pray,	7. But when you fast,
8. don't let your left hand know what your right hand is doing,	8. go into your room and shut the door	8. anoint your head and wash your face,
9. so that your alms may be in secret;	9. so that your praying† may be in secret;	9. so that your fasting† may be in secret;
10. and your Father who sees in secret	10. and your Father who sees in secret	10. and your Father who sees in secret
11. will reward you.	11. will reward you.	11. will reward you.

—Matthew 6:2-6, 16-18

This teaching in triplicate is an excellent instance of the operation of the rule of three in the shaping of oral tradition, three examples being considered sufficient to justify an unlimited extension of the basic principle to other situations. The triptych also illustrates the dexterous creation of hyperbole, along with the vivid use of both auditory (the trumpets) and visual (the doleful face) images. The very perfection of symmetry aids the student both in discerning accretions and in penetrating to the original intention in spite of accretions which obscure it.

The three stanzas deal directly with three forms of piety which had become traditional in the Jewish milieu. The actions described were presumed to be typical of the synagogues and the street corners in Israel. The teaching would have been quite ineffective had these three virtues not been legitimate goals of ambitious leaders. The majority was habitually inclined to praise those who were most generous in philanthropy and most devout in prayer and fasting, and such praise was sought by the leaders as verification of their godliness. The very strength of these status symbols is reflected in the caricatures, for the charge of hypocrisy would lose its cogency apart from the realities of public veneration. It is hard for modern readers to comprehend how offensive this attack originally was, for these three types of practice have largely lost their prestige value.

THE SYMMETRICAL FEATURES

1. Perhaps the first thing to note is the fact that lines 1 are precisely parallel to one another and also to lines 7, except for variation in the connective particles and for the different kinds of piety. To begin six successive sentences with such similar sounds facilitates memorization and suggests an original unity of intention. There is, to be sure, a minor variation in the type of Greek clause used in lines 7, but the variation is readily explained by syntactical demands which do not alter the meaning.

2. Even more noteworthy is the complete identity in Greek of lines 5 and 6. This identity extends throughout the whole textual tradition. The recurrence of this accent establishes the unity of the triptych and also suggests some significant connections with 5:21-48, where a similar saying is used six times.

3. It is impossible to overlook the congruence of lines 10 and 11 in each stanza. C 10 does, to be sure, exhibit some variation in the Greek, depending on which manuscript an editor follows, but this variation does not noticeably change the meaning. These lines are, in turn, the precise opposites of lines 5 and 6. These contrasts serve to accentuate the choice between a reward from humans and a reward from the Father.

4. This option is shown to be the direct consequence of another option: the desire "to be seen and praised" by people

versus the desire for the action to be in secret. Again there are verbal variations, but the impressive thing is the basic similarity of lines 9 and their equally basic opposition to lines 4. These lines represent the decisive issue, since the alternatives in lines 6 and 11 are the direct consequence of these motive-actions in lines 4 and 9.

5. There is, finally, an important similarity in lines 2 in the prohibition of hypocrisy. The similarity disappears in lines 3, but it becomes all the more prominent in lines 4. Hypocrisy is here defined as any intentional action which simultaneously seeks God's approval and peoples' praise. The teaching underscores not only the hypocrisy of such action, but its futility as well. Desires for human and divine praise are declared to be mutually exclusive.

Finally we notice that none of the lines in the three stanzas is expendable, although certain words may be superfluous and in a single case (vs. 17) a whole clause may be. The symmetries are bound together into a tightly knit unity which tends to resist change, whether in oral or in written transmission.

GUIDELINES FOR INTERPRETATION

The teaching provides clear clues to the stance of both teacher and audience. A single teacher is envisaged, one who speaks with authority and knowledge. Lines 5, 6, 10, and 11 take for granted that he has access to knowledge about how human and divine rewards are conferred. If people have secrets, he knows them; if God has secrets, he knows them also. He can even announce as certain the action of "your Father." The sententious character of lines 5 bespeaks an emphasis strong enough to counter any opposite assumption concerning rewards from people. It is taken for granted that the authority of this speaker rightly extends over such central religious duties as the three named, and by implication over other duties as well. Located in the Sermon on the Mount, the triptych is of course attributed to Jesus. But when one considers the status and function implicitly accorded to the speaker, it becomes virtually impossible to imagine that the early Christian church would attribute it to any other author.

Equally important inferences may be definitely drawn regarding the audience. It is assumed that this audience recognizes the right of its teacher to set the norms for their behavior. It is also assumed that they have accepted an obligation to act as loyal children of the Father and that these filial-paternal bonds are of the most intimate and secret kind. The shift from the plurals in lines 5 to the singulars in lines 7 signifies the existence of a community in which the norms for individual behavior are established and recognized. By their nature, secret actions are highly individualized; yet this teacher is addressing a group of individuals who are bound together by their loyalty to him and by their sonship to the same Father. The teaching as a whole is addressed to the whole people, yet each command can be obeyed only by each individual.

With a slighter degree of plausibility we may draw a further inference concerning the plural *you* of lines 5. This audience addressed by Jesus may represent the smaller band of disciples in their special role as pacesetters in piety, as the scribes and catechists of the Christian community. Matthew's Gospel, following the practice of Mark, normally distinguished the twelve disciples (*mathetai*) from the larger crowds (*ochloi*) of followers, a distinction roughly parallel to the contrast between the leaders (scribes, prophets, and wise men, 23:34) in the Matthean church and the more numerous laity. The disciples were visualized by Matthew as teachers-elect, doing their intern training under Jesus' tutelage; parallel to them were the Pharisaic leaders of the synagogues, who had defaulted on their assigned duties. These intern teachers were being indoctrinated into a higher standard of righteousness (5:19-20) for the sake of all the children of their Father.

What inference may be drawn from the harsh reference to the hypocrites in the negative half of each stanza? The strength of these prohibitions would be proportionate to the audience desire to dissociate itself from this particular group of hypocrites. The identity of the group is entirely clear: They are models of piety in the synagogue who have succeeded in winning the veneration of the wider public. They and their admirers assume that this veneration and God's praise are entirely complementary. However, it must be noted that the command is directed neither toward the Pharisees nor toward their followers, but rather toward competing leaders and their followers. Only in these terms would the negative commands elicit a strong impulse toward obedience. Without much doubt the triptych was shaped originally in a polemical situation, where the teaching was reinforced by existing hostility toward a group of "hypocrites" whose authority over communal behavior has been repudiated.

This polemical feature, however, can easily be misconstrued. The teaching is not in itself a weapon to be used in warfare against the Pharisees. The whole accent falls rather on the positive behavior of Jesus' own followers. The triptych was shaped to secure pedagogical rather than polemic results. The supreme danger and the alternative opportunity are those which confront Christ's disciples. The central thrust is directed toward producing a piety which is wholly secret. To seek superiority over the Pharisees would be as dubious a contradiction of lines 7 to 11 as to seek public recognition for one's goodness. The command aims at behavior that would make quite unthinkable the comparative judgments on which hypocrisy thrives and without which it dies. Individuals cannot obey this triple demand and continue either to seek or to claim superiority over their religious adversaries.

Exegetes may also easily misconstrue the polemic as a weapon in the struggle between religious institutions. They may infer that Jesus here repudiated the Jewish practices and forms in favor of alternative Christian forms (cf. Didache XI). But the three stanzas in themselves, excluding of course verses 7 to 15, do not support this. In fact, they assume that hypocrites cannot be distinguished from non-hypocrites merely by reference to varying forms or practices. The only presupposition in this regard is conveyed by the conditional clause, "When you give alms..." The character of obedience is such that it cannot be detected or measured either by opposition to all public praying, charity, and fasting, or by the cultivation of these. Rather, by repudiating all group estimates of holiness, this triad is equally destructive of both reactionary and revolutionary programs. The reason for this is made perfectly clear by the structure itself in the decisive importance which it gives to lines 4 and 9:

> that they may be seen by men…,
> that your praying may be in secret….

The inescapable issue for every person with respect to his or her own situation, whatever that may be in terms of formal religious affiliation, is the choice between these two desires, followed by their embodiment in appropriate action.

THEOLOGICAL IMPLICATIONS

What inferences may be drawn concerning the vision of God which is native to the command itself? No doubt is left concerning the desires of that God. God hates hypocrisy and requires unconditional and uncompromised integrity. God discerns hypocrisy in the deepest roots of a person's action, where desires for social recognition have their birth. If a person seeks praise from both humans and God, he or she may succeed in one but will fail in the other, for God rejects religious prestige and social honor as marks of conformity to God's will. Usually religious people, and not least their leaders, rely upon the existence of a kind of God who enforces the ethos which is rejected here. So this command poses a conflict between two gods, one of whom it declares to be false. False is the god who legislates a set of religious duties, establishes a community to observe them, enables that community to identify its rewards with his, and then encourages individual leaders to seek those rewards as the divinely authorized road to salvation. By its radical repudiation of most gods, this command discloses what is meant by trust in the gospel (Mark 1:15).

This triptych defines very precisely and very inclusively the nature of hypocrisy, by reference to the relationships pertaining between the God who sees in secret and God's children whose intentions and actions are in secret. Hypocrites are not

God's children; God is not their Father. People are God's children only when their acts of charity are hidden from themselves (cf. 6:2-4 with Matthew 25:31-46), only when their prayer to God is unpolluted by pretensions to piety, only when their fasting is invisibly inseparable from rejoicing. At the secret place where such integrity emerges one finds both God's paternal action and their filial response. The secret merging of their action with God's illustrates the mysterious interconnections between transcendence and immanence. Any notion of the covenant between God and children which encourages the hypocrisy of lines 2 is false theology. It operates with an understanding of God's omniscience which is quite different from that embodied in lines 10 and 11. It expects a set of divine rewards (cf. line 3) and thereby reflects false conceptions of God's omnipotence. It locates God's primary presence not in a person's heart, where the concept of omnipresence belongs, but in the prevailing cultural and religious customs and/or standards of judgment. In short, hypocrites (lines 2) operate with a theology which they deeply believe to be true but which is actually false.

Hypocrites operate as well with a false anthropology, a false conception of sonship. They are of course unconscious of this, and their careful observance of the demands of righteousness only deepens their unawareness. From this standpoint, religious institutions foster self-deception. Even when these institutions discourage the more obvious kinds of ostentatious piety and ambitious quests for prestige, the desire to be seen by people can subtly insinuate itself into the holiest moment. Moreover, we must recall that the forms of piety pictured in the triptych are intended to suggest many types of human behavior, whether secular or religious. These types may change from culture to culture, from century to century, but desires for social approval remain constant. By attacking those desires at the point of their ultimate theological legitimation, Jesus' demand undermines the mythological sanctions which support all social structures, whether avowedly religious or not.

There is more here, however, than an abstract notion of

humankind and of society. There is a sustained and well-planned strategy to transform "men" from hypocrites into "sons." Who can claim to be free from that form of hypocrisy which is defined here? For those who cannot, the teaching is a call to repentance, a call which opens the way to restoration of the integrity of true selfhood. This call can become a force creative of the new person, whose purity of heart enables him or her to see in secret the God who also sees in secret. No other reward is needed by God's children than to become God's children (Matthew 5:48). Here again we may see how repentance and trust are conjoined and how humankind's action indicates the fullness of the time and the approach of God's kingly authority (Mark 1:15).

What may one deduce about Christology from this triptych? First, line 5—"Truly, I say to you"—is an assertion of authority by a teacher who claims to know whereof he speaks. Also in lines 10-11—"your Father will reward"—he asserts without qualification his knowledge of God's action. This claim to authority is advanced with the presumed consent of the audience, at least that audience which has endorsed the value of the three stanzas by remembering them. Moreover, we may note that such a teacher must secure this endorsement in ways consistent with the logic of the teaching. Extrinsic social plaudits are ruled out as evidence or proof of his authority. If this teacher had sought to legitimize his status by public actions of charity or fasting, not only would he have contradicted himself, he would have proved himself the greatest hypocrite of all. The only road to legitimacy must be one which respects this "blood test" of paternity. Christ could command such behavior from his followers, and he could ground that command in an announcement of the good news and in his knowledge of God's will, but he could not vindicate that knowledge by signs which would convince the public of his own piety or power.

Efforts to describe Christ's uniqueness as Son of God should not dissolve the bonds of solidarity either with God or with the other human beings. The positive picture of intentional actions in lines 7 to 11 must be applicable to Jesus himself, or else the whole tradition of the early church would be falsified. For one whose fasting was so secret as to be hidden by joy and whose prayers were uncorrupted by public performance, his hesitation to flaunt divine authority must have been far more than calculated strategy. It must instead have been in tune with the kind of sonship-in-secret which is articulated in this triptych.

Ecclesiology is determined by Christology. The idea of church must harmonize with the idea of sonship if the church is to be considered a family. Yet, as we have noted, it is the inveterate tendency of religious institutions to use publicity to reward piety, and thus to solicit the kind of hypocrisy condemned by Jesus. No doubt the early church fell afoul of this tendency. Yet it was also the type of community which preserved these antiestablishment rules. The inner actuality of the Christian community must coincide with the inner actuality of the son-Father relationships as commanded here. The church is not truly Christ's church when it encourages the hypocrisy condemned here; it becomes the family of God only when the cohesion of its inner fabric and its standards of greatness are in harmony with the kind of invisible piety which Jesus commanded.

Supplement 3: The Expectation of Christ's Return

(These paragraphs are drawn from my book *Christian Hope and the Second Coming* [Philadelphia: Westminster Press, 1955], pp. 97-110.)

From the Sermon on the Mount on, Matthew reports that Jesus spoke of a coming day of judgment and of his own role as judge of his followers on that day (7:21-22). Each reader and each interpreter of the Gospel cannot avoid reacting in one way or another to Matthew's expectation of a return of Christ.

Was the expectation of Christ's return central or peripheral? Provisionally we conclude that neither of these alternatives is entirely satisfactory as an appraisal of the views of New Testament writers. This expectation was not by itself constitutive of Christian hope as a whole, but neither was it a marginal or accidental encumbrance on Christian life. The living Christ was himself constitutive of the hope; expectation of his final, decisive victory was an important corollary of life in him. There were sufficient varieties of expectation to furnish freedom of thought and to invite grave abuses, but sufficient common ground in the knowledge of Christ to maintain "the unity of the Spirit in the bond of peace."

Equipped with this provisional answer to the question, we move into another area, that of examining the specific predictions concerning the coming of Christ. In this task we cannot be content with sifting out a bushel of separate texts and blending them together into a formal objective statement. We quickly become aware that the terminology of the predictions constitutes a basic obstacle to understanding, since each of the key terms conveys to us a message different from its original associations. Behind this problem of terminology lies a wider problem of imagination. Biblical thought is imaginative rather than abstractly conceptual; it is poetic rather than prosaic; it is dramatic rather than static. Images native to the minds of biblical writers are far from native to ours. Nowhere is this truer than in the images associated with Christ's return. We must therefore reconceive these images in their pristine richness before we can grasp biblical terminology, and we must understand this terminology as a whole before we can justly assess the validity of the expectation. The first of these terms is that for "coming." In the phrase "the coming of Christ" the first noun is actually a highly complex image.

Fundamentalists often speak as if their "Lord" were totally absent during the interim until the great Day comes. Modernists often speak as if the presence of Christ left no place or need for the coming of that Day. Is Christ absent or present? Could he be both absent and present? To be sure, in the prosaic language of everyday conversation, when a person is present we do not think of him or her as still to come. We quite readily apply this principle to Christ. If he is yet to come, he is not now present; if he is present, it is meaningless to speak of his coming. In the language of the Bible, however, this neat division of things breaks down. The Messiah can simultaneously be both present and absent; he can be here and yet be present as one who is to come. Confusing as this language must seem, we must make an effort to understand it, for unless we do, the New Testament thought about the coming of Christ will remain contradictory or completely unintelligible.

Let us point to a few situations in which it is essential to recognize both the presence and coming of Christ if we are to cope with the realities of Christ's relationship to his disciples. We begin with the situation of prayer, hymns, and worship. The Lord's Prayer is a case in point. The address, "Our Father," presupposes consciousness of God's reality and presence, as does the doxology, "Thine *is* the kingdom." Yet the first petition (and the key one) is for the *coming* of this kingdom. Adoration, thanksgiving, confession, petition—all these imply a prior recognition of the present reality of God's glory and power. Yet they also imply the distance of human beings from God, and their dependence upon a kingdom that is both near and distant. The prayer simultaneously recognizes the nearness and the distance, but this distance is measured primarily not by space and time but by such specific concerns as the accomplishment of God's will, the gift of daily bread, the forgiveness of sins, and deliverance from the evil one.

Let us now ask *how* Jesus is present with the church and *how* he is absent. There are, of course, many different nuances in both presence and absence. One answer to this question is suggested by parables and anecdotes in the Synoptic Gospels. Jesus, being present with his disciples, gives them tasks to accomplish. Then he journeys into a far country. Or he sends them out into the villages of Israel to continue and to extend his ministry, with the assurance that he will come to them. The fact of the task presupposes that Jesus has been with them; it presupposes that in one sense (in the task itself) he accompanies them. But in another sense he departs from his disciples for the period of their work. His presence is necessary in assigning servants their posts. But his absence is also necessary if their freedom and their responsibility are to be safeguarded. The testing of their faith requires his absence, for their patience and fidelity cannot adequately be gauged unless he leaves them for what seems to them too long a period. If they must learn to carry their own crosses, they must do it when he is not there. If they are to bear the burdens of others, sweating and agonizing under the load, he must not be so near, so immediately available, as to provide an escape. Yet he remains present in the task itself—in its imperative urgency, in its ultimate claims on them, yes, even in its loneliness and apparent Godforsakenness. In his apparent deafness to their cries he may still be graciously at work for their sakes.

Why, then, do servants anticipate his return? Because the Master retains the right to an accounting. Whenever they forget this accounting, they become careless and slipshod in their work. Their mission loses both its urgency and its meaning unless it has an end. Yet when he returns it will be at an unsuspected place, in an unlikely moment, in a strange form. Only thus will his coming be a true test of their loyalty during his absence. Confidence in his risen power takes the form of alert preparedness for his return, and this readiness takes the form of total self-commitment to his commands to feed his sheep.

Still another set of connotations associated with the going and the coming of Jesus are brought to the surface by the story of Jesus' entering and leaving the temple. The meaning of his presence is clear; the significance of his exit is less obvious.

The whole Gospel narrative leads dramatically to the final visit of the Messiah to the temple, the place of prayer and the altar of sacrifice. Here the chosen people had dedicated to their God the most elaborate and beautiful building that could be constructed. In the defense of this sanctuary thousands of Jews had given their lives. Within a generation thousands more would be slain to preserve its honor and sanctity. To this heart of the nation's life came wise and devoted leaders to renew their strength in the adoration of God. They were those who defended the moral standards and the social order, decent folk obeying both religious and secular authorities. Generously they gave to the temple and its charities, ten percent or more of all they possessed. Nothing was too good for the decoration and beautification of God's holy hill. Here all the festivals of the year were celebrated in stately dignity. It was at the most sacred festival season that Jesus came to the temple. And what did he say?

"Woe to you, scribes and Pharisees, hypocrites!...You serpents, you brood of vipers...You are accursed!...How are you to escape being sentenced to hell?"

It is hard to exaggerate the consternation, the bitter sense of injustice, the angered sense of sacrilege, which must have greeted this stinging rebuke. In their minds they were far from hypocrites, nor had anyone else called them vipers. They were recognized everywhere as staunch defenders of God's own sanctuary. Such an attack as this was nothing less than a blasphemous challenge to the temple itself, and to the God who for generations had been worshiped there. And from whom did this attack come? From a Galilean troublemaker and rabble-rouser, an untrained and unlicensed layman. Here he was—a man who pardoned notorious sinners and condemned noted saints, a man who claimed that God had given him authority to break laws by which decency and order had been preserved, at great cost, for centuries.

Why, then, did Jesus turn his sharpest sarcasm at this group? He said: "You build beautiful monuments to the prophets. You decorate the graves of the martyrs." Was this the reason? Was he against the prophets? Were they venerating the wrong men? Surely not. Like his opponents, Jesus was speaking in behalf of the prophets and martyrs. By contrast, he was holding his opponents accountable for all the lynchings and crucifixions. He declared that the blood of all the prophets, from Abel to Zechariah, would be required of them.

Was the reason personal jealousy, because they held a power and prestige denied to him? Was it personal resentment, because the official leaders had made things so difficult for him? Was it vindictive hatred, because they would not recognize his credentials? If so, then he violated his own command to love one's enemies. This is just what many Jews and some Christians have concluded.

But the only trouble with this answer is that it is simply not true. Consider Jesus' lament over the Holy City: "O Jerusalem, Jerusalem, killing the prophets and stoning those who are sent to you! How often would I have gathered your children together as a hen gathers her brood under her wings, and you would not [Matt. 23:37]!" These lines are a funeral dirge in typical oriental rhythm, like a mother wailing over the body of a dead child. This does not sound like jealousy, personal resentment, blind hatred. Here is no secret gloating over the coming punishment of that child, but only deep grief on the part of a parent whose child is at the point of unwitting suicide. It was in love that Jesus cursed those whose sin had blinded them to the poisons they were drinking.

What, then, was this sin, this blindness, that was leading these good people straight to the judgment of hell? There is only one clue—or perhaps two, but they are adequate. The first lies in what these defenders of God's temple were saying *to themselves:* "If we had lived in the days of our fathers, we would not have taken part with them in shedding the blood of the prophets." There it is! It was not in building the tombs of the prophets that they sinned. Rather, it was in the self-deception of imagining that this veneration of past heroes proved their own innocence and faithfulness. What, then, might they have said? "These monuments to the prophets we have built as a memorial of our own guilt, for, had we lived in those days, we would have joined in persecuting them. This temple is a standing reminder of our own sin, built as a visible prayer to God for forgiveness. Lord, be thou merciful to us sinners!"

A second clue to their sin is this: When Jesus came into the temple, seeking penitent sinners to forgive them, these leaders were unable to say, "Blessed be he who comes in the name of the Lord!" Why couldn't they say this? Since they were unable to recognize their participation in the persecution of ancient prophets, they were also unable to recognize the word of a present-day prophet. Why should this be so? Their veneration of ancient heroes had made them confident of their own virtue. They felt certain that they could recognize a prophet when they saw him. A Messiah would surely vindicate their loyalty. Their eyes were focused upon the distant past and upon the remote future when God would welcome them as heirs of God's kingdom. When this Galilean carpenter appeared in the Holy Place, proclaiming immediate doom upon their sin, they could not bring themselves to shout, "Blessed be he who comes in the name of the Lord!" But had they viewed the temple as a sign of their own sin and blindness, had they come on that day to ask for God's forgiveness, hoping above all else to be included in God's kingdom, they would have said, "Blessed be he…" It is not strange that Jesus wept, that he called them a barren tree on which the Messiah could find no fruit.

One more question needs to be raised. What was the penalty that Jesus pronounced? What did the sentence to hell mean? Three answers are given, two in words and one in gesture:

"Behold, your house is forsaken and desolate." Forsaken by whom? By the God whose house it was supposed to be. Desolate, how? Because it was hopelessly empty. God cannot be known where there is no true repentance. God will not be a party to self-deception, but must let hypocrites alone, shut up within their self-assurance. They have their reward.

A second way of describing their penalty is this: "You will not see me again, until you say, 'Blessed be he who comes in the name of the Lord.'" The only one who can save them will not appear again until their own consciences approve his judgment and until their own hearts yearn for his forgiveness.

Jesus indicated the third penalty by a dramatic gesture: he abruptly turned and left the temple (Matthew 24:1a belongs in thought to the preceding chapter). He had come to his own, but his own had not received him. He had been eager to say to them, as to Zacchaeus, "Today salvation has come to this house." The Messiah can tarry in God's temple only when people, longing for forgiveness, are ready to listen. Until then, he must go away.

To the congregation in its worship the stories of Jesus' comings could not but have had a double meaning, for the one who had come to the disciples on a storm-tossed lake, or to a Syrophoenician woman, still had the power to come to congregations in Corinth and Rome. To them as to the Pharisees he repeatedly said, "I have not come to call the righteous, but sinners to repentance." Congregations who "built monuments" to Jesus, who sang hymns in his honor, who complacently called him Lord, needed to be reminded that this Lord could once again leave them in displeasure and in judgment. His very exit from their midst was one form of that judgment, and his return would be its visible enactment. How can those who parrot, "Lord, Lord," know that they are self-deceived unless the Lord returns with his dread verdict, "Depart from me"? To doubt his coming would leave them forever locked up with their own self-appraisal. To look forward to his coming with penitence would express dubiety over their own merit (1 Corinthians 3:5-15). Jesus Christ alone has the authority to judge. Faith in him is therefore inseparable from confidence in his coming.

Christ remains the reigning Lord. This means that he retains his power either to come to those who need him, to manifest his presence, or to depart. Either his presence or his absence is a token of his coming again. If present, he is present as a crucified Savior and Judge; if absent, it is as the same person fulfilling the same mission. Whether present or absent, he is the coming one who in coming will complete his work.

Supplement 4: The Parable of Final Judgment

(The following is an excerpt from an essay in *Theology Today* 9 [1953], pp. 489-93.)

For most readers the meaning of the parable of the sheep and the goats (25:31-46) lies on its surface, so obvious as to be platitudinous. It has been used so often in philanthropic appeals that many people, on hearing it again, instinctively clutch their pocketbooks. Because of this history, we readily assume that the primary purpose of the parable was the encouragement of altruistic impulses. A philanthropic gift is an act of kindness to Christ as well as to the needy recipient. Christ thus sanctions and sanctifies any benevolent deed.

More discerning readers detect a second "moral," a deeper level of relevance. The parable places a premium upon *unconscious* goodness (like 6:2-4), and sounds an abrupt warning against sins of which a person is *unaware*. The parable discloses the self-deception that lurks so easily behind charity. The teacher is not giving a blanket approval to all charity as such; rather he is encouraging a secret integrity, a goodness that is untarnished by either self-consciousness or ostentation. "*When* did we see thee hungry?"

Two observations may be made concerning these interpretations. In the first place, they assume that the central purpose of a parable is to give greater emphasis to a moral injunction by clothing it in symbolic language. In the second place, they treat the location of the parable in the Gospel record as virtually unimportant. The moment we substitute contrary assumptions for these, new vistas of meaning emerge. Let us assume for the moment that the primary function of this parable is to confront its hearers with the possibility of a new relationship to God, a relationship mediated by the Son of man and fulfilled in the midst of today's normal routines. And let us assume that Matthew's editor had his own reasons for placing the parable in the given context. What now happens to the basic connotations?

Let us observe several features about the context. The parable provides the conclusion to a long address, the fifth of the major sermons of Jesus and the last before the Passion. At this concluding session of his "class" the teacher has concentrated on coming events. He has tried to prepare his companions for his death, the interval of absence, and the reunion. The site of the address—how allusive it is!—is the Mount of Olives, overlooking the Holy City. One is meant to think of many other mountains in Israelite sagas. This is the place where two days later the same teacher is arrested and the same students flee. "After two days the Passover"—our parable is a link in the chain that includes the eucharist, the Gethsemane struggle, the Golgotha triumph. The parable is itself an echo of the new covenant, pointing both to the Lord's death and to his coming again. The teacher knows that the period of his absence will confront them with an extraordinary kind of temptation. The whole series of parables (25:1-46) seeks to arm them for the dangers of the interim, whether Jesus is pictured as householder, bridegroom, landowner, or shepherd. The temptations will not end until the teacher returns to conduct his "final examination."

Absence has this virtue: It has a way of reducing the absentee to the status of an idea. The person becomes dependent upon our recollection of him, and this recollection becomes dependent upon a thousand factors in our "real present." Now we can substitute our *notion* of the person for the person himself, just as we live more comfortably with the thought of humanity than with a given cantankerous specimen, just as we sentimentally exalt the nature of love all the while we deny its concrete demands, so, too, disciples find the idea of their Master more congenial than his presence. The disciple does not openly disavow his teacher, nor forget his law of love. But he is inclined to offer eulogies instead of love, to prefer abstract feelings of goodwill to the more painful risks of direct action, to limit his affections to the fellows of his own circle. With this self-deception is associated another. We assume that our recollection of Jesus is so accurate that we will easily recognize him if and when he returns. He, for his part, will recognize us and honor our loyalty. Thus, hope can become as self-centered as memory. And both may claim their toll of complacency, blindness, priggishness. These qualities do more than alienate us from our brothers and sisters; they raise high barriers between us and God.

How, then, does the parable protect the disciple from betraying his Lord? By making it clear that the absent Lord is present in a disguise. His presence consists in much more than a fading memory, an abstract idea, or a heroic stereotype. He visits us as "one of the least of these," a person whose reality cannot be contested. He identifies himself first of all not with me but with my neighbor. He destroys the self-centeredness of my world by the abruptness with which the neighbor invades my island of consciousness. The genuineness of my memory of Jesus is measured by my response to this neighbor. Only when the Lord is absent can people love him by loving their neighbors. And this love is best attested when the neighbor is "one of the least."

This last phrase, so often quoted and misquoted, will bear more than casual notice. Who are the least? The common equivalent is the neediest. Why? Because the parable has become the property of benevolent institutions. To be sure, nakedness and hunger are elemental realities that claim space on any benevolence budget. To send a basket at Christmas to one of the city's neediest families is worthy of praise. It is also both a respectable and a safe gesture, because the list of families has been carefully screened to eliminate unworthy cases. But a family considered *worthy* by the world is not yet eligible for the adjective *least*. Jesus' parable does not measure leastness in terms of economic destitution alone, but includes social ostracism as well. There are sick people; in the Bible sickness connotes sin and contagion. There are naked people; in the Bible nakedness connotes guilt and disgrace. More important still, the parable mentions aliens and convicts. The *least* are folk who are ostracized, who possess no significance, prestige, or power. Matthew and his first readers would have included wandering Christian prophets, imprisoned by their enemies (10:16-23; 24:9-14). To visit *them* in prison makes one a social deviate, an offense to respectable folk. To identify oneself with them is to share all the hostility and danger in which they stood. This is one reason why the parable belongs so near the Passion. The least are those people with whom the Son of man identified himself: the hopeless, the helpless, the exiles, the lepers. The upshot of that identification was that he himself became "despised and rejected of men." His death and resurrection reveal the meaning of that identification, while the new covenant in his blood becomes the bond uniting him with his servants. Those servants, when imprisoned and threatened by martyrdom, became "the least of these," authentic representatives of this martyr.

One further implication of the parable may be noted. There are preachers who use this story with gusto even though they reject as outmoded any thought of the Lord's return. The maker of the parable, however, clearly thought otherwise. He suggests that the Lord is now present in three different respects: *as memory*, the recollection of a Nazarene who taught this parable and died on a cross; *as hope*, the anticipation of a final accounting and a final reunion to share in "the joy of the Lord"; *as "one of the least of these."* The parable assumes that each of these three is essential. Its authority derives from its author, the Son of man who saved through suffering; without this authority the parable might convey lofty moral sentiments but not the demand of the Most High God. Even this authority, however, can be diluted into a vague, self-centered concept. From such a danger the disciple is saved by the intervention into his private world of "one of the least." This present situation provides a test of loyalty to the hidden Son of man. But this in itself is not the end of the matter. The results of this test are not accessible to the disciple. His own estimate is vulnerable, as is that of his neighbor. Only the Son of man is qualified to pronounce, "Well done" and to extend the invitation, "Come." Unless he returns, the thought of identifying him with "the least" remains nothing more than an interesting and edifying idea. The validity of such an idea could never be established. Faith in his return is evidence that we have to deal with a person and not merely with an abstract idea. When the Son of man comes he will surprise everyone, either with the unexpected rigor or with the unexpected mercy of his verdict, or with both. This Judge, however, will be the same person who has earlier identified himself with "the least of these," and who, earlier still, has exemplified the divine mercy both in his parable and in his Passion.

Supplement 5: The Covenant and Great Commission

(The following is an excerpt from my chapter in *Missions Under the Cross,* ed. N. Goodall [London: 1953], pp. 64-80.)

The covenant in Christ...the commission from Christ... There is no halo around these words. *Covenant* may denote a bargain among suspicious competitors; *commission* may indicate a salesperson's rate of profit. We must go much deeper than the words. The words themselves but point to a tightly woven web of tapestried experience. A genuine covenant is the actualized fusion of wills, the existential action that links together the source and the goals of human decisions, the hidden structure of historical events. As a word, covenant is a concept that is much neater and thinner than the historical process itself. But as the structure of creation, covenant points to God's awesome and tremendous activity, pervading all ceaseless coming and going of human generations.

Speaking of this depth-dimension of human existence, we may say that whatever genuine vocation there may be is dependent wholly upon God's covenant with the people; whatever genuine covenant there may be is dependent upon God's promise. Mission, covenant, promise—all are dependent upon God's faithfulness. That God is faithful is the gist of God's message in Christ.

The whole of the Gospel story is a direct sequel to the promises of God to Israel. The genealogies of Jesus underscore the fact that all generations share in this consummation. The birth narratives announce a God-sent governor, an Emmanuel who shall save God's people from their sins. Deliverance from the hand of our enemies is the boon granted through John the Baptist. God fulfills the pledge to Abraham by raising up sons for Abraham "of these stones" (3:9), and from all the tribes of earth (Acts 3:25). So faithful is God to promises that God sends healing and peace first to Israel, to whom belong the sonship, the glory, the covenants, the giving of the law, the worship and the promises (Romans 9:4). Though they have become God's enemies, God treats them as beloved for the sake of their forefathers (Romans 11:28). God sends the Son from the realm of promise into the realm of frustration and endows this Son with the Holy Spirit, the active power of the coming kingdom. God commissions him to herald the dawn, to heal the sick, to cast out demons, to cleanse lepers. Freely this Pioneer of the Coming Age dispenses its blessedness to the blind and the paralyzed, the centurions and harlots. Even to a gentile, God offers, on the basis of faith alone, a seat at the messianic feast with the patriarchs (8:11). Faith, expressed in repentance and its works, is proper and sufficient response to this promise.

The age of the law and prophets had lasted until John; since then, the age of redemption has invaded the present evil age. Jesus points to its signs, its power, its forgiveness, its authority over Satan. These are all pure gifts, in accordance with God's pledges. Fellowship, joy, and peace are all miracles that come from the other side of judgment, from that sphere where all things are being made new. Among these gifts, inseparable from their joy and power, is an assignment for Jesus' disciples. We should not forget that there was a commission before the Great Commission. After they have joined Jesus in the *kairos* of feasting and joy, he trusts them with his own authority and sends them as newscasters through village and countryside (chap. 10). They are sent, like him, to the lost sheep, the outcast, the poor, the despairing sinners in Israel. First, Jesus had been sent as missioner. Now, they are sent as his messengers. They extend his ministry of overcoming fears, sickness, sin, the demons, and death. When they are arrested as troublemakers, the Holy Spirit empowers and speaks through them. Losing their lives en route, they are assured of the glorious appearing of the Son of man. Thus, for both the Messiah and his servants, the dawning of the age of promise brings a career of humble, love-impelled ministry. In their work, God confronts people with promised redemption; in the response to their work, people accept or reject God's invitation. This is the surprising way in which God had chosen to accomplish the creative plan.

The new covenant in Jesus' blood serves as the necessary basis of the Great Commission. Just as the mission of Israel was dependent upon the Sinai covenant, so the task of the church is grounded in the Passion cup. It was in his death that Jesus appointed to his disciples a covenant, a kingdom, a table. It was in his exaltation that they became aware of this covenant as mission. They are visited by the crucified Lord. And everywhere in the New Testament this visit means a vocation. The exaltation of Jesus is commission. The commission is exaltation.

Thus the words in Matthew 28:16-20 are much more than a command. They are first of all a great proclamation: "All authority in heaven and on earth has been given to me." To be sure, this delegation of authority is still hidden from all but the disciples. That is why their task is to tell others how God has given to the crucified power over every enemy. In the end, every eye shall see his glory. In the interim, the work of the church is valid only to the extent that it demonstrates this basic truth: Christ is now the head of every principality and power, the Lord of all lords in heaven and earth.

The Great Commission is, in the second place, a great promise, not of something far away, but of something nearer than hands and feet. "I will be with you even to the end of the age"; from Calvary to Parousia. His presence will be hidden, of course, but all the more real. *How* will he be with them? In the guise of those whom they are called to serve: the naked, the hungry, the sick, the exiles, the prisoners (25:31-46). *Where* will he meet them? Around the table; often this table will be in the house of the despised and the unclean. His guests will be the nobodies brought in from the highways. *Who* is it who will be with them? One who has himself been naked, hungry, a prisoner, a condemned traitor; one who blessed lepers and harlots, and pronounced terrible woes and lamented over the Holy City, the temple, the synagogue leaders; one who poured out his blood "for many for the forgiveness of sins." Where he is, there is God's kingdom and power, the Spirit and its gifts. In him God fulfills all promises. In him is a promise by which all his disciples are sustained: "I will be with you."

Finally, this commission is a set of marching orders from this companion. "Make disciples of all nations." This appears to include two activities: baptizing and teaching. Such a baptism (from Jordan to Calvary) can only be carried out through the name and power of the Trinity: the Father who alone recognized the Son when no person could identify the carpenter of Nazareth as Savior of the world; the Father whom only this Son can reveal to us, and that only by dying in the form of a Servant; the Spirit who, coming upon Jesus at his baptism, drove him into the wilderness, led him through fearful trials, gave him healing words to speak, invested in him the authority and joys of the new creation. To be baptized into the name of Jesus means to die with him and to rise with him, to be marked as his possession. It means that their mission is nothing less than the work of the all-powerful, the all-knowing, the all-loving.

Disciples must be taught as well as baptized. What does this mean? To them must be mediated the promises, the covenant, the commission, which Jesus gave to his first followers. Every disciple must become a son who knows what his Father is doing; must become a slave who awaits the return of his Lord, alert, expectant, patient, confident; must learn to interpret the law and the prophets as Jesus did; to interpret the tradition of Jesus' words in the light of that truth that was in Jesus; must have his mind shaped by that covenant of life that was made available to all people in his death. This, then is our commission: to baptize and to teach.

The covenant makes clear that a basic motive for accepting the commission is gratitude. The covenant is called a eucharist, and this applies to both the thanks given by Jesus and the thanks given by his disciples. We are inclined to minimize the power of this gratitude. To indicate its radical character, let us recall the situation in Paul's day. The conflict between Jews and gentiles was just as bitter as anything we have seen. The present hostilities between East and West are short-lived in comparison with that ancient feud. Yet this thickest of walls tumbled like the walls of Jericho before the new Joshua's trumpet. Gentiles who had detested Israel became sons of Abraham, and gloried in their new heritage. Jews who had loathed gentiles eagerly visited them with an invitation to enter the holy household of faith. To do this could mean death for either Jewish apostle or gentile convert. How, then, could this mission be accomplished? The miracle did not come through obeying the same law, nor through their becoming a part of the same race. The miracle transpired through their receiving a portion of God's love in Christ. God had included them in promises to Abraham, had invited them to drink a new covenant and to live by a new law. Total gratitude enabled them to break the bonds of ancestral human traditions and to accept a new life continuous only with the promises of God and the faith of Abraham. Their gratitude was so great that every obligation was a joy. The Great Commission sent enemies to minister, to suffer and to die, for enemies.

Supplement 6: *J.S. Bach's Interpretation of the Matthean Passion*

(The following is excerpted from a longer essay in *Theology Today* 30 [1973], pp. 243-55.)

Picture by picture, Bach the interpreter follows the episodes narrated by Matthew the Evangelist, recording in music the impact of each episode on his mind. The initial chorale is typical. Here tenor and baritone have made the ominous announcement that the Son of man will be delivered up to be crucified (26:1-2). Because of the familiarity of that prediction, the casual or conventional reader usually allows it merely to graze the edge of his or her awareness, but not so with Bach. As in the case of Matthew, he and his audience knew what would follow. The announcement triggers an emotional revulsion which finds expression in the protest of the chorale. There is no verbal link between announcement and chorale, but only an explosive reaction to the situation: "Dearest Jesus, what crime have you committed that such cruel judgment is spoken against you?" This protest reflects the affection which bound the group of disciples to their Lord, their unshakable confidence in his innocence, and their horror at the cruel injustice of his crucifixion. In all three respects, Bach has surely read correctly the intention of the Evangelist and the response of Matthew's initial audience; he has made explicit an emotional vehemence which was only implicit in Matthew's more austere words.

The same emotional vehemence pervades Bach's next comment, which constitutes his reaction to the account of the priest's plot and of the anointing of Jesus at Bethany (26:3-13). From many items in the narrative Bach chooses only two for musical comment, both of which express powerful forces at work in the inner struggle of disciples. Because it is the woman's act which discloses those forces, this double comment is assigned to an alto soloist. The first notes the callous folly of the men, the second the silent gesture of the woman. Although the third person is used for both disciples and woman, the song shifts to the second person to enable the soloist (and thereby the audience) to identify herself with the woman. "Let my overflowing tears anoint your head."

Like Matthew, Bach viewed the events of the Passion with undiluted realism. The story of Jesus is taken to be thoroughly historical, profoundly human. Like Matthew, Bach was deeply concerned with the story of the disciples, who were by no means lifeless puppets, but men moved by strong forces of love and hate, pity and terror. Like Matthew, Bach saw mirrored in the twelve disciples the face of contemporary Christian congregations. All this is clearly illustrated in the musical response to Jesus' announcement at the Passover table: "One of you will betray me [26:21]."

Here Bach distinguishes the response of two groups. The disciples burst forth in frenetic, defensive denials in which, quite literally "one after another," we hear eleven repetitions of the query, "Is it I, Lord?" Few passages so effectively communicate the confusion and the tension of the original scene. In sharp contrast comes the quiet, contrite testimony of the congregation in the confessional chorale: "It is I who should do penance, and hand and foot be bound in hell." Christ's innocence discloses the Christian's guilt, his self-giving discloses their egoism, his agony their ease: "The scourges...that you have borne, my soul has earned." In this chorale the sorrow of the disciples (26:22) is expounded, albeit more fully than in Matthew, and that sorrow is accepted by the congregation as it sings its familiar chorale.

Part I of the Passion closes with the account of the arrest.

The true climax of this section, however, is the story of Jesus with his disciples on the Mount of Olives and in their Gethsemane dialogues. Neither Matthew nor Bach identified the work of atonement solely with the event of Jesus' death. Gethsemane was the locale of mortal strife where the soul of Jesus became "very sorrowful, even unto death." Here the musical comment becomes most extensive and most intense. Here the tortures of hell had struck the hardest, and help had seemed most distant. Here Bach utilized every form of comment to suggest multiple circles of meaning. The daughter of Zion exclaims over the extremity of pain: "He suffers all the tortures of hell." The "faithful" acknowledge their guilt: "My sins have struck you." In a recitative, a soloist discloses the connection between Jesus' falling on his knees before the Father and Adam's fall in which all have fallen, together with the connection between Jesus' sufferings and our restoration to God's grace. Jesus' fall to the ground is also seen as a demand for "swollen pride" to fall in humility. Arias affirm the congregation's readiness to share the cup and the cross with Jesus.

Most moving of all are three chorales which are used to interpret the Gethsemane struggle and its fruit. One chorale develops the theme of the shepherd's goodness to the sheep of the flock (26:31), a song which, like the text itself, looks beyond momentary scattering of the sheep. Another echoes the promise of Peter not to deny the Master: "I will not abandon you," and identifies every believer with Peter's good intentions. The third echoes the prayer of Jesus by reflecting on the assurance that whoever trusts in God will never be forsaken. The music expresses the mysterious ambivalence of betrayal and faithfulness, the abysses separating good intentions from evil consequences. No actor in the story escapes condemnation, and none stands outside the circle of God's mercy.

In response to Pilate's invitation for Jesus to defend himself (27:14), Jesus gave no answer, and in the next chorale Bach interprets that silence. It was a sign of Jesus' trust in God, his commitment of his "path" to God. Jesus discerned the radical difference between the *Landpfleger* (governor of the country) and the *Pfleger* (governor), who rules the heavens and who is always faithful in guiding the paths of humans. Jesus chose to commit himself to the only Judge who judges justly (the chorale is reminiscent of 1 Peter 2:23 and 4:19), and the silence before Pilate disclosed that commitment. His example constitutes an imperious demand for every Christian to commit his or her path "to the faithful care of him who rules the heavens," and he offers adequate proof that this ruler will guide his or her steps aright.

The emphasis upon the exemplary value of Jesus' death by no means contradicts or diminishes its atoning efficacy. One chorale makes this quite explicit: "The Lord, the Righteous One, atones for the guilt of his servant," a comment on 27:22. More emphatic as evidence is the use of Paul Gerhardt's famous hymn "O sacred head, now wounded." No fewer than five verses of this chorale are used in the Passion. Originally a secular love song, the tune had been adopted for church use in 1613 and had become one of Paul Gerhardt's lenten chorales in 1656. The words can be traced back to St. Bernard of Clairvaux. Bach's use of them in his comment on the mockery by the soliders (27:27-30) reflects keen sensitivity to the images and ironies of the original narrative. Here the paradoxes of the situation find apt musical expression.

To Bach as well as Matthew, Jesus' death meant a unique disclosure of God's redemption; yet to both writers the death of Jesus conveyed the demand for every follower to carry his or her own cross (16:24). Limited as he was to the text of the Passion story, Bach finds this imperative concealed in the episode of Simon of Cyrene (27:32). His example covers many types of cross-bearing and suggests their disciplinary value: "Surely will the flesh and blood in us be subdued on the cross; the more good to our souls, the more bitter the contest." Unlike Simon, the believer wills to carry this cross himself or herself, although he or she is also certain that for such a burden help will be needed: "If my suffering one day becomes too heavy, then help me to bear it myself." Here Bach surely adds a notion not intended by Matthew, although it expresses a profound insight into the mystery of Christian endurance.

For both Matthew and Bach the last enemy is death, and the fear of death derives its power from sin; the example of Jesus' victory over death becomes a supreme paradigm of the victory available to the Christian. Jesus' death and the Christian's death are simultaneous realities. The trial of the Christian consists, at least in part, of the uncertainty whether in dying he or she will be separated from Christ. So in the chorale which accompanies the expiration of Jesus (27:50), the members of the congregation join in singing their own prayer *in extremis:*

> When I die, do not depart from me!
> When I must suffer death, draw me to you!
> When my heart comes near its final anguish,
> Wrest me from distress by virtue of your distress
> and pain!

BIBLIOGRAPHY

Benjamin W. Bacon, *Studies in Matthew*. New York: Holt, Rinehart & Winston, 1930.

Gunther Bornkamm, et al., *Tradition and Interpretation in Matthew*. Philadelphia: Westminster Press, 1963.

W.D. Davies, *The Setting of the Sermon on the Mount*. New York: Cambridge University Press, 1964.

Floyd V. Filson, *Commentary on the Gospel According to St. Matthew*. New York: Harper & Row, 1960.

Martin Franzmann, *Follow Me*. St. Louis: Concordia, 1961.

H. Benedict Green, *The Gospel According to Matthew in the Revised Standard Version*. New York: Oxford University Press, 1975.

S.E. Johnson, "The Gospel According to St. Matthew," in *Interpreter's Bible*, edited by George A. Buttrick. Nashville: Abingdon Press, 1951, Vol. VII.

G.D. Kilpatrick, *The Origins of the Gospel According to St. Matthew*. New York: Oxford University Press, 1950.

Beda Rigaux, *The Testimony of St. Matthew*. Chicago: Franciscan Herald Press, 1968.

J. Rohde, *Rediscovering the Teachings of the Evangelists*. London: SCM Press, 1968.

Eduard Schweizer, *The Good News According to Matthew*, translated by David E. Green. Atlanta: John Knox Press, 1975.

Krister Stendahl, *The School of St. Matthew*, Upsala: C.W.K. Gleerup, 1954,

M. Jack Suggs, *Wisdom, Christology, and Law in Matthew's Gospel*. Cambridge, MA: Harvard University Press, 1970.

W. Trilling, *The Gospel According to St. Matthew*. London: Burns & Oates Ltd., 1969.

MATTHEW
The Teacher's Gospel

Paul S. Minear

"Most studies of Matthew have been oriented toward a
recovery of the portrait of Jesus or toward strengthening
faith in him in our time. I have chosen a different
orientation. The focus of my attention is on the work of the
Evangelist as a teacher and on his intended audience in the
churches of the first century—men and women who, like
many of us, were charged with basic educational work
among adult believers in Jesus Christ. I hope that such an
orientation may strengthen your sense of kinship both with
the Evangelist, who was a teacher, and with his first
readers, who also were teachers."

—From the Preface

This insightful commentary on the Gospel of Matthew will
help readers better understand the importance of this book
of the New Testament. Paul S. Minear focuses on Matthew
as a teacher in the early Christian church; assesses
Matthew's impact on Christians in the first century; and
examines the fascinating array of literary forms found in this
Gospel. Throughout, the book aims at increasing
comprehension of the distinctive and constructive
theological stance of Matthew.

*Paul S. Minear, an ordained minister in the United Church
of Christ, is Winkley Professor of Biblical Theology
Emeritus at the Yale University Divinity School. He is the
author of many books, including* Images of the Church in
the New Testament, Christian Hope and the Second
Coming, *and* The Gospel of Mark.

The Pilgrim Press
New York

$7.95

ISBN 0-8298-0617-2

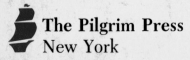